Youth with Alcohol and Drug Addiction

Escape from Bondage

HELPING YOUTH WITH MENTAL, PHYSICAL, AND SOCIAL CHALLENGES

Title List

Youth Coping with Teen Pregnancy:
Growing Up Fast

Youth Who Are Gifted:
Integrating Talents and Intelligence

Youth with Aggression Issues:
Bullying and Violence

Youth with Alcohol and Drug Addiction:
Escape from Bondage

Youth with Asperger's Syndrome:
A Different Drummer

Youth with Bipolar Disorder: Achieving Stability

Youth with Cancer: Facing the Shadows

Youth with Conduct Disorder:
In Trouble with the World

Youth with Cultural/Language Differences:
Interpreting an Alien World

Youth with Depression and Anxiety:
Moods That Overwhelm

Youth with Eating Disorders:
When Food Is an Enemy

Youth with Gender Issues: Seeking an Identity

Youth with HIV/AIDS: Living with the Diagnosis

Youth with Impulse-Control Disorders:
On the Spur of the Moment

Youth with Juvenile Schizophrenia:
The Search for Reality

YOUTH WITH ALCOHOL AND
DRUG ADDICTION

Escape from
Bondage

by Kenneth McIntosh
and Phyllis Livingston

Mason Crest Publishers
Philadelphia

Mason Crest Publishers Inc.
370 Reed Road
Broomall, Pennsylvania 19008
(866) MCP-BOOK (toll free)
www.masoncrest.com

15 14 13 12 11 10   9 8 7 6 5 4 3 2

ISBN 978-1-4222-0133-6 (series)

Library of Congress Cataloging-in-Publication Data

McIntosh, Kenneth, 1959–

  Youth with alcohol and drug addiction : escape from bondage / by Kenneth McIntosh and Phyllis Livingston.

      p. cm. — (Helping youth with mental, physical, and social challenges)

  Includes bibliographical references and index.

  ISBN 978-1-4222-0143-5

  1. Youth—Drug use—United States—Juvenile literature. 2. Youth—Alcohol use—United States—Juvenile literature. 3. Youth—United States—Social conditions—Juvenile literature. I. Livingston, Phyllis, 1957– II. Title.

HV5824.Y68M395 2008

616.8600835—dc22

2006022557

Interior pages produced by
Harding House Publishing Service, Inc.
www.hardinghousepages.com
Interior design by MK Bassett-Harvey.
Cover design by MK Bassett-Harvey.
Cover Illustration by Keith Rosko.
Printed in the Hashemite Kingdom of Jordan.

The creators of this book have made every effort to provide accurate information, but it should not be used as a substitute for the help and services of trained professionals.

Contents

Introduction 6

1. High Times 9

2. Close Call 29

3. My Name Is Sam 43

4. Point-Blank Range 53

5. It Hits the Fan 77

6. Struggling Toward Freedom 89

7. Dashed Hopes 101

8. Showtime 111

Glossary 119

Further Reading 121

For More Information 121

Bibliography 124

Index 125

Picture Credits 127

Author and Consultant Biographies 128

Introduction

We are all people first, before anything else. Our shared humanity is more important than the impressions we give to each other by how we look, how we learn, or how we act. Each of us is worthy simply because we are all part of the human race. Though we are all different in many ways, we can celebrate our differences as well as our similarities.

In this book series, you will read about many young people with various special needs that impact their lives in different ways. The disabilities are not *who* the people are, but the disabilities are an important characteristic of each person. When we recognize that we all have differing needs, we can grow toward greater awareness and tolerance of each other. Just as important, we can learn to accept our differences.

Not all young people with a disability are the same as the persons in the stories. But you will learn from these stories how a special need impacts a young person, as well as his or her family and friends. The story will help you understand differences better and appreciate how differences make us all stronger and better.

—*Cindy Croft, M.A.Ed.*

Did you know that as many as 8 percent of teens experience anxiety or depression, and as many as 70 to 90 percent will use substances such as alcohol or illicit drugs at some time? Other young people are living with life-threatening diseases including HIV infection and cancer, as well as chronic psychiatric conditions such as bipolar disease and schizophrenia. Still other teens have the challenge of being "different" from peers because they are intellectually gifted, are from another culture, or have trouble controlling their behavior or socializing with others. All youth with challenges experience additional stresses compared to their typical peers. The good news is that there are many resources and supports available to help these young people, as well as their friends and families.

The stories contained in each book of this series also contain factual information that will enhance your own understanding of the particular condition being presented. If you or someone you know is struggling with a similar condition or experience, this series can give you important information about where and how you can get help. After reading these stories, we hope that you will be more open to the differences you encounter in your peers and more willing to get to know others who are "different."
—*Carolyn Bridgemohan, M.D.*

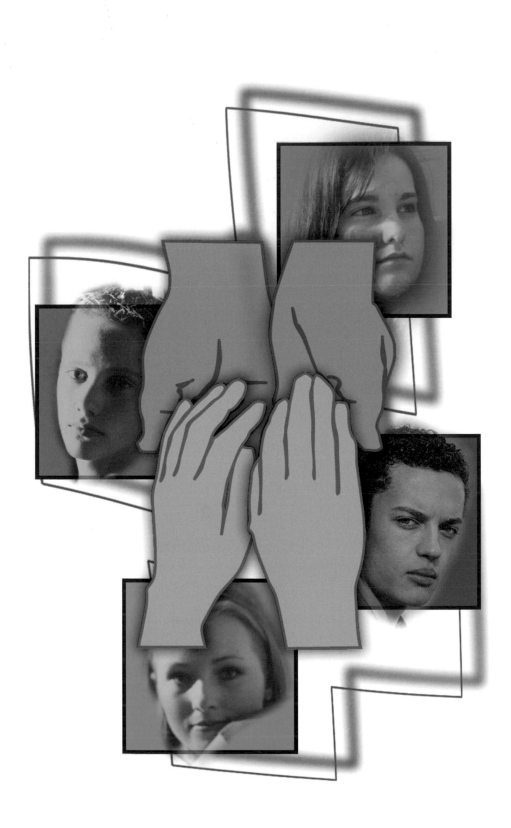

Chapter 1
High Times

t's a Saturday afternoon and we're jamming in my living room. The name of our band is written in big letters sprayed onto the vibrating head of the drum set: *Impulse!* The rhythm rushes through my body as I caress the strings on the Fender, then surges through cables to the amplifier, and explodes out of two big Peavey speakers. There's an odd hum coming out of the monitor and the C chord sounds a bit flat, but who cares?

I look around at the guys in the band and imagine how I might introduce each of them at a major concert: "Ladies and gentlemen, behind me on the drum set, the big kid with the heavy beat, give it up for—Stevie Corwin!" I can hear the applause in my imagination.

"To my right, the little guy with long red hair and glazed expression, on bass, that freaking guitar idol, put your hands together for—'Buzz' Thomas!" More loud applause.

"And to my left, massaging those keys on the Yamaha synthesizer, let's hear it for—John Carduci!" The fans cheer.

And my introduction? The scene shifts, and I imagine myself on a late-night television talk show. The host stands up behind his big desk and says, "We have a special guest tonight, the leader of that sensational new band *Impulse!* from Huntington Beach, California, give a big warm welcome to—Jason Hughes!" In my mind, I walk out onto the set as the audience cheers, my lanky limbs in black jeans, T-shirt, and jacket, my hair long and dark, and the shadow of a beard over my chin and cheeks. In my daydream, I seat myself in the host's big chair, looking all relaxed.

"Jason, to what do you attribute your amazing success?"

I tell the imaginary talk show host, "Well, the music makes people feel happier and gives them hope that things can be better."

And this much of my day dream is true: music can do wonders. When my father left us six years ago, it wasn't

Mom that got me through all the pain—she was too busy taking comfort from a bottle. No, it was the Kinks' *Sleep-walker* album, an old vinyl LP that I bought at a used music store for two dollars. Ray Davies sang, "I'm your brother" and promised that together we could find a way through troubles. It wasn't just the words but the heart in his voice that encouraged me. And there were a lot of other "broth-ers"—from the Grateful Dead to Elvis Costello, from the Ramones to Nirvana and Sublime—they all help me through tough situations. What have I learned in my time on this planet so far? Life stinks, parents and friends may be shaky, but music—*genuine* music that goes right to your soul—you can always count on that.

Someday when *Impulse!* is famous, there will be some poor little snot-faced kid sitting alone in his bedroom cry-ing because his dad's an uncaring jerk and his mother's passed out on the sofa, and he'll think "No one gives a rip about me." Then he'll hear my voice on the radio, and it'll give him what he needs to make it through another lousy day. So I have to make it big—for him.

Back to reality, Mom sits across the room on the sofa, smiling at us with a glass full of Smirnoff in her hand.

I remember one day in class at Shore View High when the teacher asked what our parents did for a living. One kid says, "My dad works for CyberDream developing soft-ware."

The girl next to him says, "My mom's a professional photographer."

And the next student: "My folks own the Tiki Treasures gift shop on Main Street."

The teacher looks at me. "Jason, what about your parents?"

It's just after lunch hour, and I toked up a few minutes ago, so my judgment is a bit off; I give him the straight-up honest answer. "My mom lives off the divorce money from my dad, who's a rich prick and never calls me. She sits around the house and drinks booze."

The class just stares at me in silence.

I can't relate to the stuff other kids say about dealing with their parents: they have to be home at a certain time, get hassled for poor grades, and they sneak around to smoke or party. I don't ever remember Mom telling me not to do something; I drift through the house as she makes vodkas disappear and flirts with her boyfriend-of-the-week. Other kids say, "Jason, your mom is a dream!" but sometimes I wish Mom would give me just one order, or yell and get mad at me. Mom acts more like a teenager than I do, and I wonder: does she really care at all about me?

Before practice today, I smoked a bowl of weed, hydroponic—good stuff. When I want to get seriously high, I do smack, but pot is useful to stay in a happy mood while I'm working on my musical skills or getting through school.

Being high might explain why I'm having trouble with this rehearsal; I just can't seem to get the old six-string in tune.

Suddenly, the drumbeat stops. Stevie throws his drumsticks on the floor. The three of us turn to face him.

"You guys sound like crap!" Stevie yells. This is kind of scary. With his girth, an angry Stevie is an imposing sight. "I'm on beat, but none of you are in the groove with me."

Buzz yells back, "That's crazy."

"No, it's not. Jason's guitar is completely out of tune, John's in the wrong key, and Buzz, I don't think you're even playing the same song as the rest of us."

Buzz starts to swell his chest out like he's gonna blow up in Stevie's face, so I say something to try and lighten the situation. "Chill, guys—we sound all right to me." Sometimes I lie a little.

John says, "I think the problem is we're not in the right mood—let's take a break."

We put down our instruments, but Stevie is still hyperventilating and looks reddish.

"Hey, Mom," I say, "we're going out back."

She smiles. "Fine, Jason, I have to freshen up a bit 'cause Charley's coming over."

I don't know who Charley is and I don't ask. We head out the back door.

There's this little porch behind the house that provides protection from any prying eyes. Beneath it are a picnic table, benches, and a mini-bar. We open the mini-bar but it isn't filled with drinks: it's our stash. John and I pull out a bag of brown smack, some tin foil, and a glass tube. Buzz pulls out a syringe, swabs, and a bottle of rubbing alcohol; Stevie looks at him with disgust.

We heat the powder; I hold the foil and John holds a lighter beneath it, while Buzz retracts the plunger of his syringe. Stevie turns his back to us and puts his head in his hands. Then John and I take turns holding the foil as we smoke smack through the glass tube while Buzz swabs his arm with the cotton and shoots up.

I've shot up a few times in the past, but I prefer to smoke or just inhale the stuff. Once when I was a little kid, I passed out in a doctor's office when the nurse tried to take a blood sample from my arm; I still don't like to poke myself with sharp objects. On the other hand, the more I smoke smack the less high I get, and that's why guys like Buzz who've been taking it for a couple of years prefer the syringe; it's definitely a better high.

Stevie looks over his shoulder at Buzz, and his eyes focus on the needle where it enters the little guy's skin. "That's disgusting!"

Buzz comes back at him with, "You're an idiot—always putting someone else down 'cause you're afraid to have a good time."

Stevie shakes his head. "This band is pathetic—talking about how we're gonna be so great and awesome but every practice you three get stoned."

Buzz is unfazed. "You're way too serious, Stevie. You need to try this sometime. It'll make you smarter—happier too."

"Buzz, I'd rather lick a toilet in one of those bathrooms beneath the pier than stick that needle in my body."

I get into the discussion, then. "It's part of the scene, Stevie—you know that. All the great musicians, they do this stuff."

"Yeah?" Stevie comes back. "Think about Jim Morrison, Jimmy Hendrix, Jerry Garcia, Brad Nowell—where are they now?"

"They're immortal gods enshrined in rock heaven," I tell him.

Stevie is not amused. He stares at me like his eyes are going to jump out of his pudgy face and says, "Jason, you'll never see the success you dream about because the drugs are ruining your music. And I'll tell you what really kills me: *you could be great.* You have this incredible talent and you're throwing it away for this!" Stevie picks up Buzz's syringe, then tosses it on the table and stomps out of the yard.

"Screw him," says Buzz.

John says, "Your guitar did sound a bit funny today, Jason."

I'm starting to drift, so it's hard to focus on the conversation. "The . . . uh . . . the strings kept moving on me."

"Yeah. . . ," Buzz says. "They . . . ah . . . do that you know?"

I'm watching the palms in the yard; they're quivering in a funny way. Pretty cool. But there's this nagging thought in my head: Stevie's a good friend. Why's he so mad with me?

Whoa. Now the trees are spinning in a circle.

I'm lying in bed now: Buzz and John finally stumbled home, but I still feel happy and awake from that smack. And when I don't think about music, I dream about Vanna.

Have you ever met the perfect girl? I have. Her name is Vanna Khan, and she's a junior at Shore View High. Her parents came from Cambodia, and she has exquisite exotic features: wide, dark eyes you can stare into and be lost forever, and a smile so big it could bring happiness to the entire world. She's petite but angled perfectly in all the right places—long legs, thin waist, and perfectly rounded breasts. Vanna is proof to the world that there is a God—or at least a goddess.

Crazy thing is, I want a girl I'm not sure will have me. We live in two different worlds, like Romeo and Juliet. I'm part of the stoner tribe. We wear ratty old clothes, don't worry about grooming except for piercings or tattoos or cool stuff like that, and we're not really into school. Vanna, on the other hand, is a socialite. If her jeans are patched and torn, it's because some designer for the pricey Laguna Hills clothes shop made them that way before slapping a two-hundred-dollar price tag on them. Socialites waste amazing amounts of money and time at unisex hair salons and manicure shops, but they're very conservative with body art. And they do well at school because that's their ticket to pricey colleges where they can meet wealthy spouses and breed the next generation of spoiled socialite kids. Like I said: different worlds.

The drugs are another thing that separates us. They're a big part of my life but Vanna's real straight edge. She might sip a glass of wine, but that's the most I've ever heard of her having to do with what you could call a "substance."

What chance do I have to win Vanna's heart? Ah! The golden key to everything—music! I remember the night when heaven touched earth at one of our shows. The set was drifting off into a hypnotic jam thing; Stevie was circling around the cymbals and snares, John and Buzz playing little riffs off each other, and I was dancing with the mike stand. The crowd was swaying, all contented looking and then—I saw her! The rest of the room disappeared as my mental spotlights shone on a single figure, her flawless body swaying like the beauty of music itself. And then she looked at me and gave this big smile. My legs melted; I had to lean on the microphone stand to stay on my feet. I knew then that music was the way to worship my goddess.

Since then, she's been dropping little spots of sunshine in my path. She'll float past my locker and lightly run her finger over my shoulder, a touch of pure bliss that leaves me trembling, trying to catch my breath. Or she'll walk past me in the hallway and say, "Hello, Jason" in an alluring way that could just as well be "Jason, I want you." I am definitely on her radar, and that's enough to make me get up every morning and face the new day.

Getting sleepy now. . . . The stuff's wearing off. Starting to dream. . .

I walk through fog. I see a girl coming toward me, surrounded by a warm aura of light. She takes my arm in her hands, and her huge eyes gaze at me with admiration. My whole body pulsates with warmth and happiness.

Huh? Another pair of hands grabs my left arm, but these are ice cold. I turn and see another woman, but this one is totally different from the first one. Her skin is white, powdery. Her face is beautiful but cold, even scornful. And her eyes . . . they suck at my soul even as they strike terror to my heart.

I hear Vanna's voice on one side of me. "Jason, I want to be with you. Make that other woman go away."

The ice woman answers, "Shut up you, little tramp, Jason is *mine*. He can't say no to me even if he wants to. I'm in his veins, every day. He'll crumble if he leaves me. I own his money, his talent, his very soul."

The two girls pull at me from opposite directions, but it's no contest. Vanna has no physical strength; the ice woman has a grip of iron. She wrenches me away from Vanna and whirls me off into thick mist. I hear Vanna call after me, but her voice fades.

The ice woman is alluring, breathtaking, but then I look again at her face. No! The beautiful features are gone, replaced with death's ghastly mask. She laughs mockingly. "You're mine, Jason. You've given yourself to me, and it's too late to turn back now." She absorbs my whole being into her deathly whiteness.

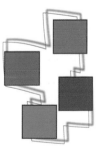

Why Do Kids Use Drugs and Alcohol?

The U.S. Department of Health and Human Services' Substance Abuse and Mental Health Services Administration (SAMHSA) estimates that 26 percent of persons twelve years old and older currently smoke cigarettes (one out of four people, including teens). Despite the fact that underage drinking is illegal, 18 percent of those between the ages of twelve and seventeen currently drink alcohol (nearly one in five teens). Sixty-one percent, or nearly two out of three,

In this group of six teenagers, odds are that one or two of them are regular drinkers.

young adults between the ages of eighteen and twenty-five are current regular drinkers. The 2002 National Survey on Drug Use and Health found that 20 percent of teenagers ages twelve to seventeen (one out of five youths) and nearly 54 percent of young adults ages eighteen to twenty-five have used marijuana. The same study also reported that use of cocaine, heroin, Ecstasy, and prescription drug abuse continued to rise in 2002 in both age groups. Despite decades of educational *initiatives* and prevention programs, teens are still smoking, drinking, and doing drugs. Why?

According to the Canadian Centre on Substance Abuse, a study conducted among college students in 2004 found that 32.0 percent of undergraduates could be classified as hazardous/harmful drinkers. Slightly more than half (16.1 percent) were heavy-frequent drinkers. Tobacco products were smoked by 12.7 percent of undergraduates. The same study indicated that 32.1 percent of college undergraduates in Canada smoked marijuana at least once during the previous twelve months. Almost 9 percent had used another illicit drug during the same period.

Five Reasons Teens Try Drugs

1. Low self-esteem

2. Social pressure

3. To satisfy curiosity

4. To escape family problems

5. To alleviate boredom or emotional pain

The reasons behind a teen's choice to smoke, drink, or use drugs vary as much as teenagers themselves. In general, however, these six factors seem to be most instrumental in steering a teen's decision away from or toward substance abuse:

- family influence

- peer influence

- circumstantial pressures

- pleasure-seeking

- curiosity/boredom

- biological/psychological factors.

Family Influence

When a young person's parents abuse an addictive substance, she grows up with role models who imply that using alcohol or drugs, even in excess, is an acceptable part of family life. Research indicates that 80 percent of children's values, morals, and attitudes are formed by the time they reach eight years of age. Siblings, cousins, parents, aunts, uncles, grandparents—all can greatly influence a teen's decision about drugs, alcohol, and tobacco.

But family influence doesn't have to be negative. A 2002 study released by the National Institute of Child Health and Human Development revealed that parental involvement in early adolescence can actually overcome peer influence when it comes to smoking. Researchers found that teens whose parents were involved in their lives were less likely

A teenager who grows up seeing her parents abuse alcohol is more likely to see this as acceptable behavior.

to start smoking than teens who did not experience much parental involvement, regardless of whether or not their parents were smokers. Involvement, not smoking status, influenced teens more.

Not every kid who comes from a smoking or drug-abusing family becomes a smoker or an addict, however, nor does every kid from a nonusing family stay clean. Something beyond family influences must impact a teen's choice to do drugs.

Peer Influence

Many teens will tell you that friends are the most important thing in their lives. Having friends, being accepted, fitting in, being liked—these are all very real needs for all people, even grown-ups, but these

Peer pressure plays an important role in most teenagers' lives. If their friends drink, they are more likely to do so as well.

needs are especially important for teenagers. The less confident a teenager is about who he is and what he believes, the more pressure he's likely to feel to be like everyone else.

Circumstantial Pressures

The National Institute on Drug Abuse identifies parental issues, ready drug availability, and poverty— all circumstantial pressures—as three key factors that put a teen at high risk for choosing to do drugs. Problems like parental issues and poverty give teens reasons to want to escape. Without drug availability, teens would be unable to get the drugs they wanted, even if they wanted them.

"Bad" circumstances aren't the only circumstances that drive teens to try drugs, including tobacco and alcohol. The pressure to perform in sports can lead to drug use. (Think of the track star who uses steroids to boost performance.) Heavy academic loads can push overachieving teens to use drug substances to improve the clarity of their thinking. (Think of a student chugging caffeinated drinks to stay up all night studying for an exam.) The desire to work harder or faster or longer can lead to using **stimulants** that push the body beyond its bounds.

Pleasure-Seeking

Many abused substances make you feel wonderful, if only for a short while. These substances often affect the pleasure centers of the brain, creating unnatural feelings of wellness, happiness, and **euphoria**, called a "high."

Curiosity, boredom, and rebellion are normal aspects of any teenager's life—but these normal emotions can sometimes inspire dangerous behaviors.

Curiosity, Boredom, or the Desire to Rebel

Many teens begin using drugs or other substances because they are bored and want some excitement in their lives. Some experiment with drugs because they're curious about what the substances will do to them. Others start as a way to rebel against their parents or as a means to test their limits.

Adolescence is naturally a time of growing up and becoming more independent. It means discovering who you are and what you can do. Part of this normal discovery process includes a lessening of parental control and a testing of established boundaries. Some teens choose to test the boundaries in constructive, positive ways: they push themselves in sports; they pursue higher academic standards; they become involved in community service, or take on a challenging job. Others test the boundaries with clothing styles, body piercings, tattoos, or statements of personal identity. Still others push the envelope with behavior: arguing, staying out late, slacking off in school, lying, or experimenting with sex. But for some, substance abuse is their statement of independence. By using drugs they are saying in effect, "See! I can do what I want, and you can't stop me."

Chapter 2
Close Call

t's a bright blue California afternoon as I saunter toward home after school. I smoked a joint in the parking lot with John as soon as school got out, so I have a pleasant buzz going. I turn the corner onto Westphalia Lane where my house is and. . .

Oh crap. No way. I freeze in my tracks; my heart skips a beat. I don't believe this.

In our driveway I see two blue and white cars with red lights on the top. This is for sure not a social visit.

Now what? Should I run? Where would that put me? I can just imagine the headlines: *ASPIRING TEEN ROCK STAR HIDING FROM THE LAW. Anyone knowing the whereabouts of Jason Hughes should contact the Huntington Beach Police Department immediately.*

No, running is not a good long-term option. But I just toked up, and if they give me a drug test now, I'm going to register on the "high-as-a-kite" scale. I sweat as I force myself toward the house. This must be how convicts at San Quentin feel on their way to the gas chamber.

I walk to the front door; my hand takes the knob on the security screen door and pulls it open. Into the death chamber; will I get any last requests?

Freaky scene. Mom sits on the couch. Clothes disheveled. She cries. Hands cuffed. An officer sits on the other end of the sofa taking notes as he talks to her quietly.

In a chair on the other side of the room is some guy I've never seen before. He looks a bit like the Bay Watch dude, wearing a turtleneck and suit coat, but one sleeve is torn off. I'm guessing this is Charley, Mom's latest boyfriend. He is also cuffed, and he talks real loud and makes big gestures to the other cop.

The officer sitting with Mom stands up and comes over to me. "You Jason?"

By now I've figured this isn't all about me so I'm calmer.

"Yes, officer."

"Sorry to tell you this son, but your mom has gotten in trouble today."

I nod, stare at him blankly.

"She and Mr. DeVree got into an altercation in front of the house. A neighbor called us. They are both quite intoxicated. I'm sorry, but I think we're going to have to take this gentleman and your mom to the station and book them there before we can release them. She'll be cited for drunken disorderly conduct and public disturbance. You'll probably have your mom home before nightfall."

He turns back toward the couch *and then I have my second shock of the day.*

I look past the officer. Past the couch. Through the glass patio door. *Our drug paraphernalia. It's in freakin' plain sight. Right there. On top of the picnic table.*

From where I stand, I can see my glass pipe, and Buzz's needle—all the incriminating evidence you could ask for! If I can see the stuff from here, the cops can too; all they have to do is glance in that direction. If they see the paraphernalia, they'll search the back porch, where they'll find five or six bags of smack in the mini-bar. I have trouble catching my breath.

If there is a God in heaven, please don't let the cops see that stuff and I promise I'll be good from now on.

Both officers stand. The one shoves the guy in the coat ahead of him; Mr. Baywatch-star-look-alike does not go quietly. The officer with my mom pauses in front of me, and Mom tries to say a few words but she's too intoxicated.

I take her hand in mine and attempt to mumble some reassurance, but my mind is elsewhere. *Get this freaking cop out of here before he happens to look toward the patio!*

They're all out of the house, and I hear one of the police cars pull away. I sit on the couch with my head in my hands for a moment, trying to catch my breath, pull myself together. Then I stand and head toward the patio; gotta put all that stuff away ASAP. My hand is on the latch of the sliding glass door, about to open it.

"Excuse me, Jason!" My heart stops. It's the police officer calling from the front screen door. I turn around, trying not to hyperventilate and keel over.

Be calm. Speak in level voice. Don't show fear.

"Yes, officer?"

"May I have a word with you?"

This is it. Here comes my career as convicted criminal.

I open the screen door and step outside. The police officer gazes at me with a concerned expression.

"I know this experience must be very hard on you, Jason."

"Yes, sir."

"I think your mom is going to need more help than this little scare today. I'm not sure what sentencing will be, but regardless, you should encourage your mother to attend Alcoholics Anonymous. I'm afraid she has a problem."

"I'll do that, officer. Thanks."

He nods, walks back to the cruiser, and pulls out of the drive. I see Mom in the backseat of the patrol car behind the steel mesh, still crying.

I stumble back into the living room. I can't believe I haven't wet my pants. I glance back at the driveway to make sure the police are finally gone, and then I head back to the patio.

Gotta clean all this stuff up. I pick up the needle to put it away, and then I stop. My hands shake, and I know what can make me feel better. I reach in the mini-bar for a bag of heroin. I take up the foil and pull out a lighter, then put it down again.

Maybe there's a lesson here. Stevie's right: this stuff is gonna ruin my music, and it could mess up a lot of other things besides.

But I'm really hurting now, sweating and shaking all over. My hands tremble as I pour the little tan granules onto the foil and heat them. I reach for my pipe . . . no, I really feel like a wreck. I'm turning to jelly inside. I need a stronger high.

I grab Buzz's needle. Yeah, I know I shouldn't share, but Buzz is clean. Besides, the screaming pain is drowning out the rational part of me. I need smack inside of me good and fast. I swab quickly, jam the needle in my arm, push the plunger, and I'm back on my way to happy land.

Happy land? Who am I kidding? I don't control this stuff anymore; it controls me.

Why Do Some People Become Addicts—and Others Don't?

Researchers have discovered that certain people are more likely to become addicted to drugs than others because of how their bodies are wired. They have a genetic predisposition to addiction; in other words, something about their *genes* makes it easier for them to become addicted than someone with a different genetic makeup. The fact that many addictions are repeated from one generation to the next illustrates how genes can influence a person's interaction with drugs.

Medical conditions and psychological disorders can also make a person more prone to using and abusing drugs: depression, *bipolar disorder*, *schizophrenia*, *oppositional defiant disorder*, untreated attention-deficit hyperactive disorder (ADHD), *obsessive-compulsive disorder*, *post-traumatic stress disorder*, and others. The National Institutes of Mental Health (NIMH) estimates that one-third of those with depressive disorders and one-fourth of those with major depression have substance abuse problems as well.

How Do Drugs and Alcohol Affect the Human Body?

The Brain

Messages are carried within the brain by nearly 100 billion cells called neurons. Communication happens when the sending neuron, called the presynaptic neuron, sends an electrical impulse down its long, thread-like limb, called the axon, to the branches at the end of the limb, called dendrites. When the signal reaches the tip of the sending neuron's dendrites, it has to ride on special carrying chemicals called neurotransmitters, over the gap between that neuron and the others surrounding it (called the synapse) to the neuron whose job it is to receive the message, called the postsynaptic neuron. This kind of communication between neurons occurs literally billions of times per second to accomplish your bodily functions and thought processes, including everything from blowing your nose, to sleeping, to breathing, to reading a book.

For our minds and bodies to work properly, however, communication between brain cells must stay in good working order. Inhaled or ingested chemical substances alter brain chemistry, especially the neurotransmitters (how much the sending neuron

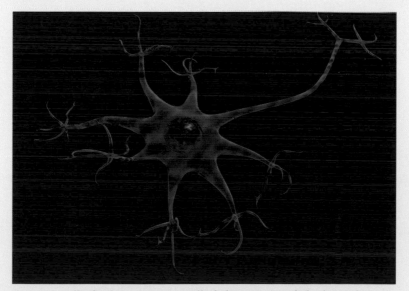

A nerve cell; the long piece is called the axon, and the branches at the end are the dendrites.

releases to carry the signal, how much is accepted by the receiving neuron, and how much stays in the synapse), and when brain chemistry is altered, neuron communication is disrupted or breaks down. And when communication between neurons breaks down, a person's thinking, feelings, and physical abilities change. Substance abuse can alter how much of these chemical messengers are produced, how they carry their messages, and whether or not they are able to deliver the message to the next cell. Different drug substances may affect different neurotransmitters, but all neurotransmitters are necessary for the brain's proper functioning.

To understand how alcohol and other chemical substances affect those who use them, we need to understand how different parts of the brain control different aspects of our bodies, minds, and emotions.

- The *cerebrum* is the largest and most important part of the brain and controls higher thoughts and reasoning, memory, voluntary movement, sensory perception (sight, sound, touch, etc.), speech, language, learning, and perception.

- The *cerebellum* is the part of the brain located beneath the cerebrum at the back of the head and controls automatic, involuntary posture, balance, and muscular coordination.

- The *brain stem* is the brain section below the cerebrum and in front of the cerebellum through which all body signals must pass to move from the spinal cord to the brain. This part of the brain controls reflexes and involuntary actions.

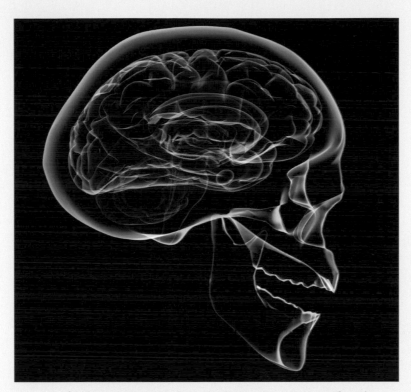

Chemical substances, including alcohol and nicotine, affect the way the brain operates.

- The *limbic system* is a group of structures that create a person's emotional makeup, including pleasure and aggression. Whenever we experience pleasurable circumstances, the limbic system releases a specific kind of neurotransmitter called "dopamine," which creates pleasurable feelings. The more dopamine released, the more pleasure we feel. Most abused chemical substances affect the limbic system, creating short-lasting feelings of pleasure called a "high."

- The *hypothalamus* is a part of the limbic system that balances overall body metabolism and regulates body temperature, emotions, hunger, thirst, and sleep patterns.

People who have had too much to drink, for example, share some typical behaviors: their speech may become slurred; they may fall down a lot; they may look hot or flushed; they may have difficulty walking or writing; they act stupid or say stupid things; they may become intensely emotional (angry, giddy, or sad); they may throw-up; they may get sleepy or pass out. All of these behaviors are rooted in alcohol's effect on the neurotransmitters in the brain, especially a single type of neurotransmitter called GABA.

Let's say that person drinks a shot of whiskey or downs a pint of beer. The beverage moves down the throat, into the stomach, and into the intestines,

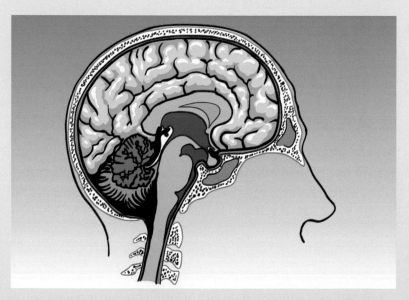

Alcohol affects all the brain's various parts: the cerebrum, limbic system, the cerebellum, the hypothalamus, and the brain stem.

where the bulk of the beverage's alcohol content is absorbed into the bloodstream (about 20 percent is absorbed into the blood while passing through the stomach; the rest is absorbed through the small intestine). The blood then carries the alcohol throughout the body (liver, kidneys, brain, etc.).

When alcohol reaches the brain it affects the cerebrum first. Since the cerebrum regulates thinking, self-control, and the ability to process sight, sound, smell, and other senses, the drunken person might first become more carefree, less reserved, and more talkative. He may have difficulty seeing or hearing well, and may not notice minor bumps, scrapes, and bruises since he isn't processing pain senses effectively. This person's ability to make good decisions, think clearly, or practice self-control may be seriously impaired. All this happens when alcohol reaches this first part of the brain.

Then the alcohol moves from the cerebrum into the limbic system. Since this set of structures controls emotional responses and memory, the person may become violently enraged or overwhelmingly sad. He may cry, throw things, or become aggressive. And he may not remember his behavior the next morning.

From the limbic system the alcohol moves into the cerebellum, which controls and coordinates muscle movements and balance. The intoxicated individual may become unsteady on his feet, lose his balance, or demonstrate stiff, jerky movements. This impact on the cerebellum is what police officers test for when they ask a suspected drunk driver to walk a straight line heel-to-toe or to touch his finger to his nose.

The alcohol continues its journey through the brain, stopping next at the hypothalamus (and the closely related pituitary gland, which controls hormone secretion). At this level of intoxication, the person may become sleepy, hungry, may need to urinate more, and may find his sexual desire has increased (although his ability to perform sexually is decreased).

Finally the alcohol arrives at the brain stem, which controls all the survival functions your body performs over which you have little conscious control: breathing, body temperature regulation, heart rate, consciousness. A person with enough alcohol in the their blood to impact brain stem function can stop breathing, experience uncontrolled blood pressure, or developing an out-of-control rise in body temperature, all of which can be fatal.

The Rest of the Body

If chemicals affected only the brain, that alone would be enough to cause serious damage, but these substances affect other parts of the body, too. How the drug is taken into the body impacts which additional parts of the body are affected.

Smoking, snorting, or inhaling will obviously irritate the nose, sinuses, airway, and lungs. Smokers develop coughs and get lung, mouth, and throat cancers. People who snort cocaine experience perpetual runny noses and chronic nosebleeds.

Substances that are ingested by swallowing, drinking, or eating (pills, liquids, laced food) irritate the linings of the stomach and intestines, can cause ulcers, and can increase blood flow to the stomach, which reduces blood flow to other parts of the body.

Virtually all chemical substances enter the bloodstream, not just those injected, so all are processed through the circulatory system (heart,

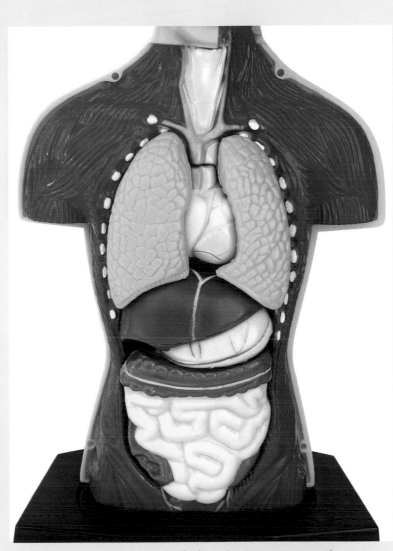

You may not usually give much thought to your internal organs—but virtually all of them are affected by any drugs or alcohol you ingest.

lungs, veins, arteries, kidneys) and pass through the body's most vital organs (including the pancreas and liver). This distribution throughout the vital organs explains liver disease in alcoholics and kidney failure in junkies.

Chapter 3
My Name Is Sam

"My name is Sam, and I'm a recovering drug addict," says the tall, middle-aged man with a long ponytail and receding hairline.

The crew and I are at a special assembly for Shore View High seniors, seated in the very back of the auditorium. That's a good thing, because Buzz giggles all through these assemblies and we don't want to get in trouble. As long as I can remember, we've been subjected to annual "Don't do drugs they're bad for you" shows. They were more fun in elementary school, because they had costumes and puppets like Sesame Street. Then in middle school, they had really crazy old movies that made drugs seem pretty interesting.

Now we just get occasional washed-out speakers who aren't so much fun.

But there's something about this guy; I feel drawn to him from his opening words. He's not trying to impress us; he doesn't sound fake or rehearsed. He's just a guy talking to this whole rowdy crowd the same way I imagine he talks to his friends in his living room.

"I grew up near here in Seal Beach in the '70s, and it was a lot of fun." He tells about his school days filled with surfing, bonfires on the beach, and fooling around with his girlfriend under the pier at night; I'm amazed they let him get away with this stuff at a school assembly. This guy is right on.

"In 1982, I had just graduated from UCLA in communications, and I got hired to work as assistant to the vice president at a major record label. That was awesome. One month, I got paid to follow this rock band around on a concert tour and arrange interviews for them—what a blast!" Sam has the crowd's attention now; can you imagine getting paid for that?

"Of course, I was into everything you imagine with the whole scene—'sex, drugs, and rock 'n' roll' as they say." Sam goes on telling of stars sniffing coke like it was candy in the 1980s, of watching hot acts ruined by drug use. The whole time, though, he assumed he could handle the stuff. "I was a user, not an addict. At least, that's what I told myself."

Funny, that's my line.

Now Sam talks about the down side of drug use. I've heard this same spiel a hundred times, but this time it sounds different. Sam tells how drugs made his career in the music business go downhill, and how they ruined his relationship with a woman named Amanda, someone he thought would be the love of his life. I can hear the pain when he tells us this. And I can relate to it; all of a sudden, I see myself on a cruise down the same dead-end road.

"Now, I'm not here to tell you what you should or shouldn't do. You guys are very close to entering full-fledged adulthood and you're not stupid. You're going to make your choices whatever I, your teachers, or your parents tell you." I like it when older adults acknowledge our ability to make independent decisions, so I keep listening.

"Today I want to address those of you who are where I was a while ago. You've already decided you want to get off the dope. You are ready to say, 'I am addicted and I really want to change.' There isn't some magic wand that will take away the craving for drugs. You'll always have to resist the pull to addiction. But I want you to know there is a proven way to get off drugs."

Sam pauses a moment, and I'm surprised to realize that I'm waiting to hear more.

"It's called NA—short for Narcotics Anonymous. Some of you are already familiar with Alcoholics Anonymous.

This is similar, but it's not focused on just one drug but on any kind of addictive substance. NA works on a simple premise: the best person to help a drug addict is another addict. As our literature says, Narcotics Anonymous is 'a society of men and women for whom drugs had become a major problem who meet regularly to help each other stay clean. We are not interested in what or how much you used but only in what you want to do about your problem and how we can help.' The recovery process happens mostly through support meetings. Again, this isn't rocket science. We just tell our stories and encourage one another."

Okay, I'm still listening, even though I don't really want to anymore.

"I'm not gonna talk much more about NA in this assembly," he says. "And again—I'm not telling you how to run your life. You have what it takes to decide all the big issues, including what kinds of substances you put in your body. But if you don't like the road you're on, and if you feel like things are getting out of control with drugs, then show up at a meeting. We'll do all we can to help you. Thank you for listening. Have a great day."

Sam heads off the stage. Buzz is giggling, "What a clown."

I feel like Buzz is in some parallel universe; this guy really spoke to me. We're heading out of the auditorium now, but I slip away from my class and double back toward the front of the room, where the speaker is picking up his things. I walk up to him.

"Hey, I'm Jason. I'm a senior here."

Sam nods and offers his hand.

"If, uh, I wanted to meet up with an NA group, where would I do that?"

"Where do you live?"

"Sea Side Gates Community."

"There's a meeting just a mile and a half from there, about five blocks in from Ocean on Main Street. Know where the Bogart Theater is?"

"Yeah."

"Meetings every day of the week, 3, 5, and 9 P.M., at the VOA office across the street from the theater."

I hesitate for a few seconds. "What'll happen if I show up? Do I have to say anything? Is it gonna be weird?"

Sam grins. "No, Jason, you don't have to do anything. Just come, listen, and share when you feel ready—no one is gonna put heavy pressure on you or make you feel uncomfortable."

"All right." I can't think what to say next, and I'm feeling pretty stupid all of a sudden. "Well . . . maybe I'll check it out."

"Great. Hope to see you there."

"Yeah."

I shake hands with Sam again and run to catch up with my class.

What Is Addiction?

Drug addiction and drug use are not degrees of the same thing. The original choice to use drugs is voluntary, and drug use can *lead* to addiction, but true addiction is never a choice. True addiction happens when drugs alter the user's brain chemistry in such a way that the brain creates a chronic, compulsive craving for the drug. Occasional drug users can quit when they want; addicts suffer from a drug-use-induced illness and cannot quit on their own.

Am I a User or an Addict?

Each of the following is a warning sign that drug use is becoming drug addiction. The more "yes" answers you have, the more likely it is that you have an addiction.

The decision to smoke your first cigarette is a voluntary choice you make.

A person who is addicted to nicotine can no longer quit smoking easily; she will probably need some type of help or support if she is to be successful.

1. Do you get drunk or high regularly?

2. Do you think about or plan your substance use in advance?

3. Do you get drunk or high alone?

4. Is using making you sick or causing you ongoing physical symptoms?

5. Do you lie about how much or how often you are using?

6. Have you stopped doing things you used to enjoy (like sports or hobbies) so that you can get drunk or high?

7. Have your eating habits, sleep patterns, or mental abilities changed? Have your grades dropped?

8. When you're not high, do you feel depressed, hopeless, run-down, or unmotivated?

9. Do you have blackouts or memory gaps?

10. Do you have to use more of the same substance to recapture your earlier highs?

Diagnosing Addiction

A recognizable pattern exists with the repeated use of many addictive substances that helps to correctly diagnose substance dependence:

1. The individual develops tolerance for the substance, meaning that she must ingest more and more of the substance in order to obtain the desired effect.

2. If a person suffering from a substance-related disorder does try to resist the substance, he often experiences a series of unpleasant withdrawal symptoms. These symptoms are usually the opposite of the experiences brought on by the substance. Withdrawal symptoms can lead a person to take more of the substance (or a closely related substance) in order to eliminate the uncomfortable feelings brought on by withdrawal symptoms.

3. It becomes progressively difficult for the individual to resist consuming the substance, even for one day. In fact, the individual may begin using the substance several times throughout the day. The individual may use the substance for a longer period of time than originally intended and in increasingly larger amounts.

4. The person becomes unable to use a limited amount of the substance even if she has set a limit for herself.

5. Although the individual sincerely wishes to do so, efforts to discontinue use or to decrease the amount of the substance used are unsuccessful.

6. More and more of the person's day may be devoted to the substance (thinking about it, finding ways to acquire it, spending time in areas where it can be used without detection, and actually using it). As a consequence, areas of the person's family and social life might be neglected, as might their employment.

7. Use of the substance continues even if the individual recognizes the negative impact it is having on his well-being, including physical (for example, liver damage caused by alcohol use, malnutrition as a result of heroin use, etc.) as well as psychological problems (for instance, depression following use of cocaine).

Chapter 4
Point-Blank Range

I decided today would be the first day of my new life, so I've gone all day without any drugs—and I'm all jittery and nervous, wanting so bad to at least smoke a joint. But I've told myself I'm going to hold off until I can check out this NA meeting that starts in just a few minutes.

I stand across the street by the theater and look at the building where they meet. Why am I so scared to walk in there? After all, I can pour my guts out on stage in front of hundreds of people when I perform with *Impulse!* so what's the big deal? Maybe I'm afraid of what it will be like if this works. I once heard an adult say that quitting smack is like getting a divorce: you may hate your partner for the way they treat you, but you're still lonely after they're gone.

I suppose I should go across the street and enter that door. *Okay, here goes.* One step toward the crosswalk, two steps . . .

A familiar Toyota Camry with tinted windows and spinner wheels pulls up right in front of me and the power window slides down. I'm looking at the driver, Marco, this twenty-something guy I get all my stuff from.

"Hey, Jason my man! Whatcha doing?"

"Nothing."

"Well then, hop in and let me give you a ride somewhere."

"No thanks."

"Uh, Jason I don't suppose you're headed for that that meeting across the street?"

How the hell did he know that? I take a deep breath. I already feel shaky, so I don't really want to get into an argument. I'm not sure about Marco. I mean he acts all nice and he's always been straight with me, but there's something crazy about the guy. It's hard to explain.

He gestures toward the empty seat. "Jump in a minute and chat with me."

I hesitate a second, but then I do as he says.

Marco pulls the car around the corner and parks behind a row of apartments. He turns to me and says, "Dude, you must be feelin' real messed up. Why you wanna go to that NA meeting? They're a bunch of losers. You're not like them, Jason. You're a user, not an abuser."

"I dunno, Marco. It's just that the whole scene—the smack, the pot—it's not working for me anymore."

"You just need to experiment some more, Jason, vary your substance routine."

"Nah, I don't think so."

"Hey, looks like you need help from an old friend." Marco pulls a bag of white smack out from under the seat and hands it to me. "Here's a bag of really good stuff. I mean this is just unbelievable, like nothing you've tried, and I'll give it to you for free."

I shake my head. "Thanks Marco, very generous, but I've gotta go."

I put my hand on the door handle but am stopped by the sound of a very loud "click." I've heard that sound before, but only in movies. I must be imagining things. I turn, very slowly, to face Marco.

Gun. Very big. In Marco's hand. I stare straight into the gaping hole in the chrome barrel, and I'm suddenly in a cold sweat; it's hard to catch my breath. But I have to stay calm ... can't panic.

"Marco, you must be kidding me. That thing's not real, is it?"

His calm reply is hardly what I expect from a man threatening me at point-blank range with a piece of artillery that would make Dirty Harry proud. "Jason my man, sometimes a dude needs a little shock, a little jolt of emotional lightning to help him reconnect everything, comprende?"

He's talking crazy. What am I supposed to say?

"Marco, tell me that's not loaded."

"But Jason, that would ruin the whole game, wouldn't it? If you thought this gun was phony, then this experience would be meaningless, wouldn't it? Maybe each chamber has a .38 magnum shell in it, and maybe if I tighten this finger a bit, your brains will go right through the window. You don't know for sure—and that's what makes this moment a once-in-a-lifetime experience, see?"

I don't see. I can't think, but I know I gotta keep Marco happy. "What do you want me to do? Just say, I'll do whatever you tell me."

He chuckles. "I think you need to take advantage of my generosity. That's really good stuff I just offered you, pure and potent. Right now, your brain is flooded with all sorts of crazy chemicals. You're all nervous, thinking, 'Maybe this is where I die.' Now, if you take a snort of that stuff right now, it'll give you a rush like you have never had in your life. So—here's a spoon, and here's the bag. Why don't you just lean back and snort some of this lovely white powder. Okay?"

I do as he says.

Marco pulls the gun back, uncocks it, and slides it in his pocket. I sink into the seat and start breathing again.

"I can't believe you did that!"

"Jason, I'm your friend remember? Sometimes friendship requires tough love. Besides, I was just messin' with ya. There were no bullets in there."

I'm not sure I believe that. The talk about brains splattering seemed pretty earnest.

Marco gives me this big grin, like he's my best friend. "Jason, you were about to make a real mistake, about to leave behind the miracle of chemistry that releases your genius. You were looking pretty bad when I found you there on the street. Tell me the truth, dude, don't ya feel better now?"

I nod, and I really do feel better. Snorting smack takes effect real fast, and I'm feeling a lot more on top of things than I have all day.

"So admit it Jason, I did you a favor. And to show I am on your side, I'm feeling generous. Here, take the rest of the bag. No charge." He stuffs it in my pocket.

As I get out of the car, Marco says, "Adios, amigo." He glides away down the street.

I walk to a bench and sit down. The world does seem brighter—or am I just relieved to have my brains still in my head? With friends like Marco who needs enemies? But he has a point: am I sure I want to quit? It's a lot easier to keep living the way I have been.

Kids and Heroin

Most teens know that heroin (sometimes called "smack") is a dangerous drug that should be avoided, but as the price of heroin declined to only $10 a dose, its use soared among teens. At the same time, addiction to prescription painkillers increased among teens—but as teens need higher doses of these drugs to achieve a high, they often switch to heroin, which is cheaper. From 1990 to 1996 heroin use among twelfth-graders in the United States doubled. By 1999, according to the Monitoring the Future study

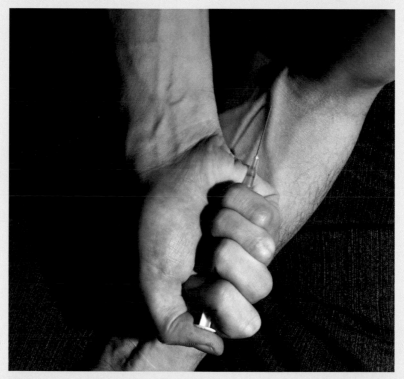

Heroin is usually injected directly into a vein with a hypodermic needle.

conducted by the National Institute on Drug Abuse (NIDA), the rates for heroin use had nearly tripled those of 1991. The average age of first-time heroin users fell from nearly twenty-seven years old in 1991 to just under eighteen years old by 1997. New heroin users are no longer adults; now they are teens.

The 2002 National Survey on Drug Use and Health revealed that roughly 3.7 million Americans age twelve and older had tried heroin at least once in their lifetimes. Nearly thirty percent of twelfth-graders said heroin was easy to obtain. Heroin, some said, was even easier to obtain than marijuana and alcohol!

How Heroin Works

Heroin is a drug that belongs to the opiate family of drugs, from which we also get opium and morphine, but it is nearly four times stronger than morphine and even more addictive. This drug's potential for abuse and addiction is so great, and its threat so dangerous, that the federal government passed laws banning it from being made in or imported to the United States.

Heroin is known as a "downer" because it suppresses brain function and interferes with the body's ability to recognize pain. It goes by many street names, including horse, smack, big H, dope, gumball, and countless others. Heroin can give a near-immediate rush when used alone, or it can be used with other drugs to enhance certain effects. Heroin used with other drugs goes by different names (speedballing, for example, is a deadly practice where heroin and cocaine are injected together).

What makes heroin so particularly dangerous is its inconsistency in dose strength, its method of use, and its power to be almost immediately addictive.

Inconsistent Dose Strength

Because heroin is made from morphine, which is made from the poppy plant, and because it is illegal in many parts of the world, heroin is manufactured in makeshift garages, laboratories, and warehouses with no safety guidelines or regulations. Heroin is illegally imported into America from other countries all over the world, so the quality of heroin varies with every dose. Some strains of heroin are so pure they can kill the junkie with one fix. Others barely give the user a high. Since there is no way to be certain of the purity of the heroin you are taking beforehand, every injection is like playing Russian roulette. You just don't know what you're getting, and you never know if it will kill you.

Method of Use

Heroin's primary means of use is by injection. Because their drive for the next fix is so strong, heroin addicts want the fastest way to get high, and injecting heroin directly into their veins is the most direct way into the users' systems. Because heroin users often share used needles, they risk sharing life-threatening blood-borne diseases like hepatitis or HIV/AIDS. Many heroin users inject themselves many times a day, and with each injection comes the risk of infection or contamination from a dirty needle.

Powerfully Addictive

Heroin is a fast-acting drug when it is injected or smoked. It can reach the brain in as little as fifteen to thirty seconds when it's injected. When smoked, the effects can be achieved in only seven seconds. The heroin high is like a rush of pleasure and good feelings—all is well with the world. The pleasure is more intense than with many other drugs because heroin is that much more powerful. With the power to be so pleasurable comes the power to be highly and quickly addictive. Many users become addicted after their first time using, and find it nearly impossible to stop.

As with other drug substances, most people on heroin need more and more of the drug to create the desired feeling. The higher the dose required,

Heroin addiction is one of the most destructive addictions; it can destroy a person's life, financially, socially, and even physically.

the more dependent the user's body becomes on the drug. The heroin user becomes trapped in a spiraling cycle of deepening addiction. Heroin is such a strong drug that with increased dosages comes the risk of taking too much. Heroin is easy to overdose. People die pursuing the heroin high because they take just a bit too much.

According to the NIDA, symptoms of heroin withdrawal can include extreme drug craving, restlessness, muscle pain, bone pain, inability to sleep, diarrhea, vomiting, cold flashes, thrashing, kicking, and very rarely, convulsions. Withdrawal symptoms reach their peak two or three days after quitting and continue in most people for about a week. For some, symptoms can last for months, but they are not considered dangerous in most cases.

Kids and Cocaine

Cocaine use among teens has been decreasing since the 1990s. This is a good trend—but teens are still trying this drug.

Some of the names teens use for cocaine:

- bad rock
- bazooka
- beam
- Bernice
- big C
- blast
- blow
- snow storm

- blizzard
- coca

Cocaine is a stimulant, the most powerful of stimulants with a natural origin; it directly affects the brain. Cocaine is not a new drug; in fact, it is one of the oldest known drugs. Cocaine is manufactured from a plant called coca leaf, which is native to the Andes Mountains of South America, where it has been ingested for thousands of years. The pure form is a chemical known as "cocaine hydrochloride," which has been an abused substance for more than a hundred years.

Cocaine is usually a white powder that is snorted up the nose.

Method of Use

Cocaine as a powder is snorted through the nose, which allows it to pass through the nasal membranes into the bloodstream. This can cause major damage to the sinus passages; it also causes teeth to decay. Injection is another way to release the drug into the bloodstream. Crack cocaine is smoked.

Many cocaine users mix other drugs together to get a better high. Speedballing, the use of cocaine and heroin mixed together, gives a euphoric feeling that is often addictive the first time it is used. Cocaine can cause arteries to spasm. If this happens to the arteries that carry blood to the heart, the user can have a heart attack.

Kids and Tobacco

According to the Centers for Disease Control and Prevention (CDC), of all young people under eighteen years of age who are alive today, more than five million will die early deaths from a smoking-related disease. Despite the widespread education of young people about the dangers of tobacco, and despite the fact that tobacco products are illegal for those under eighteen years old, more than 3,000 teens in the United States become new regular smokers *each day*. According to the CDC, tobacco use snares more than one million new users each year. Why? Because a chemical in tobacco called nicotine, a highly addictive substance, gives smokers a "kick" in a very short amount of time.

After someone inhales tobacco smoke, it takes only *eight seconds* for nicotine to reach the brain, causing an almost immediate sense of pleasure. But in less than forty minutes, more than half of the nicotine's effects are gone so the user wants to light up again to get more of the drug. In a very short time, the user's brain is so altered that she becomes addicted.

What's Really in a Cigarette?

• Dead frog preservative (formaldehyde)
• Rat poison chemicals (cyanide)
• Insecticide (nicotine)

Cigarettes and Cancer

Cigarette smoking causes 90 percent of all lung cancer cases. Cancer deaths (all kinds) are twice as high among smokers than in nonsmokers. Heavy

You might be surprised to learn what's in a cigarette!

smokers are four times more likely to die from cancer (all kinds) as nonsmokers.

Kids and Alcohol

Just because alcohol is legal for those over twenty-one years of age does not mean that it is more "safe" or less harmful than other drug substances. The Palo Alto Medical Foundation cited that on college campuses all over the United States, alcohol abuse was involved in about two-thirds of all violent behavior, nearly half of all physical injuries, about one-third of all emotional difficulties, and almost 30 percent of all academic problems. Another study done by the Nemours Foundation found that teens who drank alcohol regularly were more likely to have problems in school, to try other drugs, and to participate in

A glass of wine, a mug of beer, and a shot glass of liquor all contain about the same amount of alcohol.

delinquent behaviors such as stealing or vandalism. This study also followed these teens into adulthood and discovered that even as adults they had more difficult getting and keeping jobs, maintaining healthy relationships, had higher incidences of addiction and substance abuse, and were more likely to be involved in criminal and violent behavior.

Columbia University's National Center on Addiction and Substance Abuse found that more than five million high school students binge drink at least once a month, despite the fact that 77 percent of these students stated that they'd had at least one serious problem related to their drinking in the past year.

The severity of alcohol's effects on the body depends on how much alcohol is used, the body weight and size of the individual who is drinking, how much food is in his stomach, and how quickly the alcohol is consumed. Generally speaking, it takes only one or two standard drinks to make a teen begin to feel the effects of alcohol. Each of these contains about the same amount of alcohol:

- one twelve-ounce bottle of beer
- one twelve-ounce wine cooler
- one five-ounce glass of wine
- one and a half ounces of 80-proof liquor

Kids and Marijuana

Marijuana is the most-used illegal drug in the United States, used by more than eleven million people annually and by more than seventy-one million people over their lifetimes. It is the third-most abused substance by teenagers (after alcohol and nicotine). It can be easier to obtain than alcohol. It's made from a plant that contains more than four hundred different chemicals, and it produces another two thousand chemicals when it is burned. Some people say it's a medicinal drug and should be legalized; others say it's a dangerous, highly addictive *hallucinogen*. Despite its apparent popularity, the NIDA maintains that marijuana, though widely used among adults, is not common among teens. Fewer than one in four high school seniors currently uses marijuana according to NIDA, and fewer than one in five tenth-graders.

Marijuana use is more common among adults than teenagers.

Those who do smoke marijuana tell of a wide range of experiences when they get high. Some feel calm and relaxed; some feel very little of anything at all; others get extreme cravings for food (the "munchies"); still others experience bad highs where all they feel is fear, anxiety, and paranoia. Marijuana use increases the risk of developing a psychotic disorder, and many teens who use marijuana regularly begin to experience delusions. It is also very dangerous to drive after marijuana use, because marijuana interferes with the perception of passing time and also with how one focuses. Ironically, many teens report that they feel more focused after using marijuana, but what they likely are experiencing is the ability to have extreme focus on a *single* point—and that is not the kind of focus needed for driving!

After it has been smoked, marijuana reaches the brain within seconds and can affect the user's brain for four to six hours—a typical high. Though the effects of marijuana wear off in these few hours, traces of marijuana can be found in users' blood for days afterward. It's a highly traceable drug that accounts for many teens' failures to pass a drug test for sports or jobs.

Kids and Inhalants

"Huffing," "bagging," and "sniffing" are all terms referring to the process of inhaling chemical vapors in order to get high. The chemicals used for huffing are called inhalants. The U.S. Department of Justice estimates that inhalants are the fourth-most commonly abused substances by teenagers, following only alcohol, cigarettes, and marijuana. Because most substances used for huffing are common household products, adolescents have easy access to an unlimited supply. Most teens don't realize that huffing can kill them the first time it's tried. More than 1,000 common household products can be used as inhalants, and every one of them has the potential to kill.

Kids and Medicines That Can Be Abused

Some addictive drug substances were designed to treat specific medical conditions; they were never meant to be abused. But like all chemical substances, these drugs have the potential to alter a person's mental or physical state. And because many of these medicines are so widely available in North America, they've become a cheap, easy high for teenagers.

The National Drug Intelligence Center (NDIC) estimates that one in ten teens between the ages of twelve and seventeen have used these kinds of medicines in a nonmedical way. In other words, they've used them to get high. Another government institution, the Substance Abuse Mental Health Service Administration (SAMHSA), estimates that over five million teens and young adults used prescription medications illegally in 2001. And that number, according to SAMHSA, is rising.

In identifying which medications teen abuse most, the Partnership for a Drug Free America divides these medications into four general categories: pain relievers (also called analgesics), tranquilizers, stimulants, and sedatives.

Pain Relievers

Percocet® and OxyContin® are both prescription pain relievers. Sometimes called analgesics, the most prescribed painkillers are opioids, which come from opium, and are considered narcotics. Doctors, as this category name implies, prescribe these medicines to ease pain. For severe pain, physicians may prescribe morphine, Percocet, OxyContin, or Darvon®. For milder pain, many will prescribe codeine.

These drugs work so well in treating pain because they prevent pain messages from being received in the brain by blocking pain receptors. Like all abused substances, pain relievers alter brain chemistry in such a way that the brain not only doesn't receive pain messages, but that the pleasure center is stimulated. When abused, these drugs can produce a great sense of well-being, pleasure, and euphoria. But a single overdose of pain relievers like OxyContin can cause death from respiratory depression.

Tranquilizers

Valium®, Xanax®, Halcion®, Librium®, and ProSom® are brand-name tranquilizers that fall into the chemical family called benzodiazepines. These drugs work on the GABA neurotransmitters in the brain, slowing down brain communication and activity. Because these drugs tend to have a calming effect, they are often prescribed for things like anxiety or panic attacks, tension, stress, and sleep disorders.

When taken as prescribed, they can make a person feel sleepy, calm, or peaceful. But when taken at higher doses than doctors recommend, they can create addictions, cause seizures, suppress breathing, and slow your heart rate. Extreme overdoses or mixing these medicines with other drugs or alcohol can kill you. Withdrawal from these drugs is very dangerous and must be medically supervised.

Stimulants

Tranquilizers slow you down—but stimulants rev you up. This group of substances increases brain communication and activity by increasing the amount of the neurotransmitter dopamine in the brain, which causes greater alertness, increased ability to concentrate, better attention span, and more energy. Ritalin® (methylphenidate), a drug prescribed to treat ADHD, and Dexedrine® (dextroamphetamine) are the two stimulants teens abuse most.

When stimulants are taken too often or in too high a dose, they can cause blood pressure to skyrocket, heart and respiration rates to increase, and the body temperature to rise to dangerously high levels. They can also cause feelings of hostility and paranoia. Heart attacks and fatal seizures can occur at high doses.

Sedatives

The drugs called Nembutal® and Mebaral® are two commonly abused sedatives. Like tranquilizers, sedatives slow the body down, but unlike tranquilizers, sedatives come from a chemical family called barbiturates. Because sedatives slow down the entire central nervous system, they are sometimes called "sleeping pills."

The effect sedatives have on their users is similar to the effect caused by tranquilizers; they produce a calming effect or cause drowsiness by slowing respiration rate and acting on the brain's GABA neurotransmitters. Doctors prescribe sedatives to help patients sleep or to relieve tension or, in some cases, to make a person who is having a seizure stop convulsing.

Like tranquilizers, too much of these drugs can kill you, and mixing these drugs with alcohol can also be fatal.

Not Just Prescriptions

Prescription drugs are not the only medicines teens can abuse. Over-the-counter drugs (OTCs) like cough and cold medicines or dieting formulas can be abused as well. OTCs are perfectly legal drug substances that any teenager can buy wherever these drugs are sold. The most commonly abused OTC is any cough, cold, or flu medicine containing the chemical dextromethorphan (DXM). DXM is a cough suppressant, and when taken at higher-than-recommended doses, it can cause hallucinations and feelings of detachment from your surroundings.

Usually taken as capsules, gel caps, tablets, or syrup, DXM can cause a long-lasting high. Teens who take high doses can be under the influence of this drug six hours or more. Because their thinking and judgment are impaired for so long, these teens run great risk of injury.

DXM is safe and nonaddictive when taken as directed on the packaging label, but when abused,

DXM can cause exceptionally high fevers, vomiting, irregular heartbeat, high blood pressure, headache, numbness, loss of consciousness, seizures, brain damage, and death.

The most widely abused cough suppressant medicine that contains DXM is a product called Coricidan HBP Cough and Cold. Often called Triple C, this medication is taken by mouth and causes the same symptoms listed for DXM products. It is especially popular at all-night dance parties called raves.

Street Names for Commonly Abused Medicines

- steroids: Arnolds, gym candy, juice, pumpers, stackers, weight trainers
- Ritalin: Kibbles and bits, kiddy cocaine, skippy, smarties, Vitamin R, pineapple
- Coricidin HBP Cough & Cold Medicine: Triple C, CCC, candy, skittles, red devils
- other cough and cold medicines containing dextromethorphan: DXM, dex, Robo, Skittles, Velvet
- OxyContin: Oxy, OC, oxycotton, killers, hillbilly heroin

Kids and Club Drugs

Ecstasy is only one of several drugs called "club drugs," which are so named because of their widespread use at dance clubs and night clubs that hold all-night dance parties called raves. Raves are high-energy dances that feature pounding techno music, strobe lights, and lasers. They can be attended by as few as a handful of people to as many as thousands. Teens attending raves attempt to dance nearly all night, hours at a stretch, and often rely on chemical (that is, drug) support to maintain their energy. Club drugs are the drugs of choice for rave attendees because of the increased stamina they supply, their ready availability, and their cheap cost. This makes these drugs also particularly attractive to teens.

Rave Paraphernalia

Because of side effects from certain club drugs, teens who attend raves may bring any of these items with them:

- baby pacifiers: to protect their teeth from the grinding caused by Ecstasy
- lollipops: to suck on, again to protect their teeth from grinding
- Vicks Vapor-rub: to apply around nose and mouth to enhance Ecstasy's effects
- bottled water: to prevent dehydration from dancing
- glow-in-the-dark necklaces, pins: to enhance visual hallucinations
- Skittles or M&M candies: to hide the drugs

Rave-goers use a wide variety of club drugs, but according to the U.S. Department of Health and Human Services' National Clearinghouse for Alcohol and Drug Information (NCADI), the five most widely used club drugs are MDMA (Ecstacy), Rohypnol, Ketamine, GHB, and LSD.

Chapter 5

It Hits the Fan

This is the biggest gig *Impulse!* has ever played, and I am so nervous. Three of us are out back in the parking lot in John's car trying to get relaxed. Stevie is backstage in the club fuming about us. Buzz pulls a joint out of his pocket and passes it around. I take a few tokes. Hmm. The smoke tastes different somehow. The joint's really going to my head fast. "Hey, Buzz, where'd you get this stuff?"

"Oh, the weed is from some guy in Long Beach, grown in his greenhouse. And," he adds casually, "I mixed in a little smack from the bag in your patio."

"Buzz, you laced this joint?"

"Yeah. So?"

I say with as much enthusiasm as I can, "One—two—three," and slash at the strings with my pick. Buzz keeps pace with his bass, and I look over at John. He hesitates, listens to his monitor, and then jumps in. He's off, a full two beats behind us. Just moments into our act, we already stink.

I go on the best I can, singing with all the passion I can muster up, but this is way wrong. The crowd isn't dancing; they're just staring at us like "What is this freak show?" and I don't blame them.

We finish off the first song, and I say, "Thank you! We're *Impulse!* from Huntington Beach." The crowd stares at me. I can hear their thoughts: *Yeah? So why don't you go back there?*

We launch into our second song, and now things get weirder. My hands feel like they're disconnected from my brain. I can't make my fingers move fast enough, can't push the right strings for each chord in time. I glance over at John and see a look of pure agony on his face. He hasn't hit a key right since we got on stage. I look at Buzz; he has this zoned out look on his face as he taps on the strings randomly. We're the worst.

Somehow, we get to the end of the song. This time the crowd doesn't even pretend politeness. A girl in the front row yells, "You guys suck!" A guy chimes in, "Get off the stage so the next band can play!" and then someone starts to boo and the whole crowd joins in. It grows to a crescendo. "BOO!" "Get out!" "Go home!" I look at John, and he shrugs his shoulders. I glance toward Buzz; he grins and waves at the crowd like a total idiot, stoned out of his gourd. The room is tilting . . .

And then . . . *I see Vanna.* Just ten feet away. So gorgeous. Everyone else disappears. The world narrows down to her face, the sparks of anger in her eyes. Her mouth forms words: "You suck! Go home!"

My legs collapse, and I sink to my knees on the stage. The manager walks out, shakes my shoulder. "I think it's time for you to call it a night." I stand unsteadily and turn. *Yeah, get me out of here.* John grabs Buzz and steers him toward the back. Where's that exit? The room won't stand still. My legs won't walk straight. Ah, there's the door. Legs, go this way . . . no . . . *through* the door . . . into cool night air.

"Now what?" John says.

"Don't even tryyy to d-d-drive," I tell him.

"Nah. Too messed," he agrees.

"Catch a bus?" I ask.

"Bussss," says Buzz. I'm amazed he's that coherent.

Everything spins; street lights pulsate; why won't the world stand still? There's a bench. Sit . . . oops . . . gotta get my butt on the wood . . . there. I collapse onto the bus bench.

The scene keeps spinning. I think I'm gonna throw up. I find myself wishing the cops at the house *had* seen stuff on the back porch: then I'd be in jail now. . . . I even wish Marco had pulled the trigger on that freakin' gun and splattered my head all over the car. Any place the bullet sent me would have to be better than this. . . .

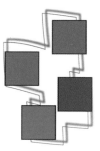

Many experts who work with people with addictions believe that "hitting bottom" is a necessary step before a person can begin to recover. In other words, a person's life must completely fall apart before he can truly accept that he needs help. As painful as this process may be, it can actually be a positive step in the individual's life.

Once the individual recognizes he has a problem, the next step is to seek help. There are a variety of options. Surprisingly, other drugs are one approach to helping people overcome their addictions.

Drugs Used to Treat Addiction

- Amantadine (Symmetrel): This medication increases dopamine activity in the brain. It has been used to treat symptoms of cocaine withdrawal and, sometimes, to help maintain remission.

- Benzodiazepines: Some of these sedatives, like Serax and Librium, are used to treat withdrawal from addictive sedatives such as alcohol.

- Buprenorphine (Subutex and Suboxone): Subutex can be used at the beginning of treatment for addiction to opiates, and Suboxone (which contains both buprenorphine and naloxone) can be used in maintenance treatment for addiction to opiates. This medication has not been tested in individuals under the age of sixteen.

- Bupropion (Wellbutrin and Zyban): antidepressants that may be used during both withdrawal and remission. Safe levels have not been established for individuals under the age of eighteen. Lithium, Zoloft, Prozac and similar antidepressants have also been used in the treatment of alcohol addiction.

- Clonidine: This nonopiate is used to treat individuals with an addiction to heroin. Safety and effectiveness have not been established for individuals under the age of twelve.

If you are a minor, your parents will be involved in many aspects of your life—but ultimately, you must decide for yourself if you are going to kick an addiction.

Doctors may prescribe a medication as part of both inpatient and outpatient treatment programs.

- Disulfiram: (Antabuse, Sulfiram): This medication is used to prevent relapse of alcohol abuse and less frequently to discourage use of cocaine.

- Methadone: Probably the most well-known opiate used to treat addiction to heroin. Levo-alpha-acetylmethadol is a longer acting form of methadone.

- Naltrexone (ReVia) and Naloxone (Narcan): These opiate-blocking drugs are sometimes used to treat individuals suffering from an overdose. Naltrexone is also used to help individuals avoid relapse by reducing cravings for cocaine, alcohol, and sometimes heroin. Safe use for individuals under the age of eighteen has not been established for naltrexone. Clinical experience regarding use of naloxone in individuals under the age of twelve is limited.

• Antabuse works in maintenance programs for alcohol addiction because the individual desires to avoid the negative consequences of using alcohol while taking this substance. An individual using this treatment option would begin taking Antabuse, either orally

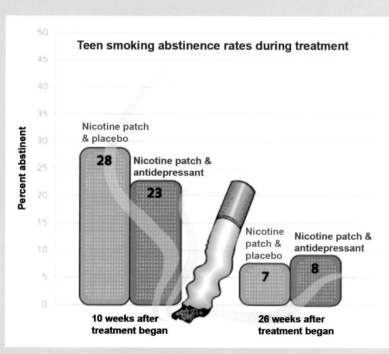

According to a study done at Stanford University, nicotine patches help adolescents quit smoking just as effectively as they aid adult smokers.

or as an implant in the body after completing withdrawal from alcohol. Unfortunately, Antabuse does not reduce a person's craving for alcohol. It does, however, interfere with the body's ability to metabolize alcohol. If a person gives in to his craving and begins to consume alcohol while taking Antabuse, a toxic substance called acetylaldehyde will begin to build up in his body. This produces uncomfortable symptoms, including nausea and vomiting. The individual's skin turns a purplish color. In severe cases, even more serious effects, including respiratory distress and heart attacks, can occur. Antabuse can be a powerful motivator for alcohol avoidance, but it has several risks. For instance, small quantities of alcohol like that found in some foods, sometimes even inhaled traces of alcohol, can induce these negative consequences. Antabuse is also sometimes effective in treating cocaine addiction, perhaps because it increases certain negative symptoms such as edginess and paranoia associated with cocaine use.

- Nicotine patches help individuals addicted to cigarettes wean themselves away from smoking.

Treatment that includes psychiatric medication must *always* be monitored by a professional who has experience in dealing with substance-related disorders.

Chapter 6

Struggling Toward Freedom

onuts are all gone, huh?"

It's Sam, the guy who spoke at our school. He's standing next to me at the table in back of the VOA hall. I've just finished listening to my third NA meeting. I say "listening" because that's all I've been doing—coming and listening to the others. I'm too embarrassed to open my mouth.

Sam says, "What do you say we walk down to Java Hut and I'll buy you a drink and a muffin?"

"Sounds great. Thanks."

We head out into the dusk and walk across the street. Main Street is glowing with fluorescent light; tourists and locals mingle on the sidewalks. Surf City would be paradise this time of year, except that I've been banished to hell.

We walk to the counter, and Sam orders two frozen mochas and two whole-grain blueberry muffins. Then we sit down at a little table on the sidewalk.

"Jason you don't look so good."

"I feel worse than I look."

"Still doing drugs?"

Something about Sam tells me I can trust him.

"Yeah. I have to smoke pot every morning to face school, and in the afternoon I snort smack."

"But you don't want to?"

That's hard to answer. "Part of me wants to—it's like the drugs are my best friends. But they're not helping me any. It's like I love 'em but I have to leave 'em or they'll ruin everything."

Sam chews his muffin. "You're still doing drugs—so why do you keep coming to NA?"

"It gives me hope."

"Hope?"

"Yeah. Everyone who stands and talks has a sad story, like you said. A lot of them are even worse than mine, because I've never lived in the gutter or overdosed. Then they say how long they've been clean. Some say "seventeen days," others say "six months," and a few say "seven years." First meeting, I thought that was bull crap. But then I listened more, and I know it's not. Somehow, these men and women found freedom. And I figure if they have, I can too. Maybe if I keep hanging around them, it'll happen to me."

Sam flashes a smile. "Right, Jason. If they're free you can be too. But it won't just happen to you—you'll have to do some things."

"What?"

"You know the Twelve Steps we recite every meeting?"

I nod.

"You have to begin walking through them."

"Yeah, that makes sense in the abstract, but what does it mean for real life? How do I do that?"

"You remember the First Step?"

"I think so. Something like, 'Admit that I'm powerless over drugs and my life is unmanageable.'"

" Yes! That's it. Jason, have you admitted both those things?"

I shrug. "If I had power over the drugs, I'd stop taking them, wouldn't I? And my life is a total mess. I think 'unmanageable' pretty much covers it."

Sam nods. "All right, that's the First Step. Just saying that shows me you're better off now than you were just weeks or months ago, when you weren't seeking any help for this problem. Now for the Second Step. Do you remember what that is?"

"Something about a higher power."

"That's right."

"What is it about this higher power stuff, anyway?"

"Well Jason, the Second Step is this: 'We came to believe that a power greater than ourselves could restore us to sanity.' Now that 'power greater than ourselves' could be anything that works for you. You already believe that NA offers a way out, even though it hasn't happened for you yet. This is exactly what the Second Step is saying—you already have come to believe that NA is a power greater than your drug addiction, and that you can be restored. Your higher power could be the group, or your philosophical beliefs, and of course for some folks in NA, God is their higher power—however they understand God."

"Yeah, higher power—I can relate to that. But is that all there is to it? I mean, if I believe in some power greater than myself, will the cravings just go away?"

"Sorry, Jason, it's not so simple. There's a lot more work you have to do."

"I guessed that." I break my muffin into pieces, and then I ask, "What comes after the Second Step?"

"We made a decision to turn our will and our lives over to the care of God, *as we understood Him.*"

"I'm not sure I get it."

"Basically, you hand your struggle over to that greater power for assistance."

"Then the higher power just does it all?"

"No. But it does that part that you can't do."

"This is a lot to absorb in one discussion."

Sam nods again. "You're right—it's too much for one day. Remember, the steps are a lifetime journey. You're just starting, so take one day at a time."

"I guess I can do that."

He smiles. "See you at the meeting tomorrow?"

"You bet."

We stand and shake hands and head out into the night, Sam toward the pier and me heading inland toward my house. As I stroll through the night air, my mind reviews all those forces that stand against me: my music career seems sunk, the one perfect girl has rejected me, my Mom's an alcoholic, my friends are all potheads, and Marco will probably try to get to me again. On top of all that, my own body is going to put me through agony when I quit taking smack. My higher power is gonna have to be really strong in order for me to handle all the challenges I'll face in the coming weeks.

Since that talk with Sam, I've gone two days without any drugs, and it's driving me crazy. I'm tense, shaky, irritable . . . my whole body craves the stuff. I go to meetings, listen to my favorite music, and hang on by a thread.

It's another Saturday morning, and what's left of *Impulse!*—me and Buzz and John—are gathered to practice. The doorbell rings, and Mom goes to answer it. She comes back with a package. "Jason, some guy named Marco says this is a gift for you." She hands me a package.

Buzz says, "Hmm . . . wonder what that is?"

I tell him, "Buzz, you know darned well what it is, and that's why it's going right into the trash."

I head for the trash can, but Buzz jumps right in front of me.

"Whoa, buddy! Just because you've given up on life's finer things, why not give it to someone else? Remember your old buddy Buzz?"

I throw him the package. "Fine. Go right down the high-way to hell—if that's what you want."

Buzz looks like a little kid who's been given a candy bar. He smiles and walks out the back door; he can't wait to take the stuff.

John looks at him and shrugs. "Let's tune up while we wait for him. I just smoked a joint so I'm fine for now."

"Yeah," I say. "Whatever." It's going to be really difficult hanging around my old friends while I form new habits.

John plunks keys on the Yamaha, and I turn the knobs on the neck of my Fender to get it in tune. Then we go through a few songs to warm up.

"Jason! Something's wrong with Buzz!" Mom's yell in-terrupts our rehearsal.

John and I run out back and see Buzz hanging like a little limp noodle over the side of a patio chair, a syringe and needle on the ground beneath his hand. I shake him and yell: no response. Feel his pulse: it's there but weak. "We've got to call 911!" but John says, "No, Jason, there's too much illegal crap in the house. Let's drive him to emergency!"

Mom says, "We'll take the Explorer. I'll drive," but I know she's already had too many drinks today so I tell her, "You can ride along, Mom, but I'll drive."

We pile into the SUV: I'm behind the wheel, Mom's shotgun, John's holding Buzz in the backseat. I hit the throttle and we fly backward out the drive; then I jam the transmission into forward, the tires squeal, and we're rocketing out of Sea Side Gates toward the main road and the hospital.

Cars and houses and phone poles whiz by the windows. We're out of our neighborhood, down the road, and almost to the turnoff for the hospital. Mom shouts, "Turn here!"

"No, Mom, it's the next turn!"

"Here!"

"No!"

Mom grabs the steering wheel and yanks. "Mom, No!"

I fight to straighten the Explorer. Over adjust. Swerve. Van in front of me. The other driver's mouth is hanging open. *WHAM!* I hear the shriek of tearing steel mixed with other screams. Then the airbags pop. And. . .

When a person wants to free himself from addiction, one of the first steps he may take is to join a program such as Alcoholics Anonymous or Narcotics Anonymous (AA or NA). Although some researchers believe that AA's success lies in the sense of support its members gain from attending regular meetings, many members, as well as AA's literature, hold that the essence of the program is the Twelve Steps.

The Twelve Steps of Alcoholics Anonymous

1. We admitted we were powerless over alcohol—that our lives had become unmanageable.

2. Came to believe that a Power greater than our-selves could restore us to sanity.

3. Made a decision to turn our will and our lives over to the care of God as we understood Him.

4. Made a searching and fearless moral inventory of ourselves.

5. Admitted to God, to ourselves, and to another human being the exact nature of our wrongs.

6. Were entirely ready to have God remove all these defects of character.

7. Humbly asked Him to remove our shortcom-ings.

8. Made a list of all persons we had harmed, and became willing to make amends to them all.

9. Made direct amends to such people wherever possible, except when to do so would injure them or others.

10. Continued to take personal inventory and when we were wrong promptly admitted it.

11. Sought through prayer and meditation to improve our conscious contact with God as we understood Him, praying only for knowledge of His will for us and the power to carry that out.

12. Having had a spiritual awakening as the result of these steps, we tried to carry this message to other alcoholics and to practice these principles in all our affairs.

Spiritual practices, including prayer and meditation, play an important part in the Twelve Steps.

AA members are encouraged to "work the Steps," usually with the guidance of a sponsor.

Most members regard attendance at AA meetings as important to their **sobriety** (although there are groups in AA made up of loners and members living in remote locations who communicate by mail and Internet). Many members with decades of continuous sobriety still go to meetings regularly.

A typical individual program of recovery for a newcomer may include:

- Above all, avoiding the first drink.

- Attendance at one or more meetings daily for ninety days or longer.

- Contact with one's sponsor daily in order to work the steps and to discuss whatever problems one may be having in one's life, problems that may, if not addressed, lead the alcoholic to take the first drink."

- Daily prayer and/or meditation, as suggested by Step 11.

- Daily attention to Step 10: "Continued to take personal inventory and when we were wrong, promptly admitted it."

- Service work, which, for the newcomer, can be as uncomplicated as making coffee at meetings, helping to set up and break down tables and chairs, etc.

The program is to be worked *daily* and done so *one day at a time.*

A common feature of AA meetings is that members are asked to speak to the group about their experience with alcoholism and recovery. However, there is no requirement to speak. Some members speak every time they are asked; others simply sit and listen in meetings for years before they say anything; some may choose never to speak.

When Is a Person Ready for Treatment?

In the book *Recovery Options: The Complete Guide*, the authors list six stages of change that define the process of recovery from use of addictive substances, and points out that an individual rarely moves through them (from precontemplation to termination) in a linear manner. According to Dr. Volpicelli, people with a substance-related disorder are much more likely to move through the stages in a cyclical manner until they achieve termination.

- Precontemplation: Giving up the substance has not yet been contemplated.

- Contemplation: The individual is thinking about the situation and deciding if she wants to stop her dependence on the substance.

- Preparation: The person is getting ready to take action.

- Action: The individual is actively engaged in discontinuing substance use.

- Maintenance: Efforts are made to sustain remission.

- Termination: A maintenance program is no longer needed.

Chapter 7
Dashed Hopes

I struggle to breathe, but my chest is on fire. Something red and sticky is obscuring my vision.

"Mom! You all right?"

"I think I broke my arm."

"John?"

"Shook up but no damage."

"How's Buzz?"

"He's still unconscious, breathing . . . can't tell anything else."

A man is screaming at me through the window, yelling profanities and shaking his fists. I realize he's the driver from the other car. He's got blood on his face and arm, but from the way he's acting he can't be hurt bad. I decide I'll just sit here 'til the cops come.

I don't have long to wait before I hear sirens wailing. Before long, a police officer taps on the window. "You hurt bad?"

I shake my head.

"The others?"

I decide it is time for some brutal honesty. "My mother's arm is hurt. I think my friend in back is more urgent, he's overdosing on heroin, and he's unconscious. I know you'll need a report on this accident, but please, right now could you just get us to the hospital? My friend may be dying."

That speech does the trick. An ambulance pulls up. They put Mom and Buzz on gurneys and wheel them into the emergency vehicle; the EMTs ask me questions about Buzz and I tell them what little I know. The officer tells us to get into her squad car so we jump in the back. The police car takes off with siren wailing, the ambulance following us, as other police arrive to take notes and pictures at the scene.

It's been four hours now since the crash. Mom isn't hurt bad at all; they took X-rays and sent her home already. I'm alone with Buzz in a room at the hospital. They tell me he's going to be all right. The EMTs in the ambulance gave him Narcan to get his system working right, but he's gotta stay in the hospital until the smack wears off. He's slipping in and out of consciousness and mumbling occasional nonsense.

Why didn't I insist on throwing that package away? Why didn't I call 911? Why did I let Mom ride along, knowing how drunk she was? I've screwed up so bad and hurt so many because of my idiot mistakes.

"Jason?"

I can't believe my eyes. "Vanna! What are you doing here?"

"I work as a candy striper on Saturdays at the hospital. What are *you* doing here?"

"My friend Buzz . . . he overdosed on drugs. I'm here waiting 'til he gets out."

"Oh." Vanna inhales. This isn't something that usually happens in her circle of friends. "Well, I'm glad it wasn't you," she says.

"It could have been me, not long ago. But I'm off drugs now."

Vanna's face brightens. "Oh Jason, I'm so glad to hear that. You know, I've always liked you, but with all your drug use, I was afraid to get close to you. Maybe we can get together sometime soon."

I see the doors to paradise swinging wide open. . . .

There's a groaning sound coming from the bed. We both glance down and see Buzz open his eyelids.

"Buzz! Good to see you awake," I tell him.

"Ooh . . . head feels like crap" he says.

"I'm not surprised," I tell him. "You've been through a drug overdose and a car crash today. I'm just glad you're alive!"

Buzz tries to sit up a little, blinks a few times, and grimaces. "Jason, that smack you gave me was all messed up— it almost killed me!"

"What?" Vanna stares at me. "Jason, you lied to me. I hate you!" Before I can explain, she spins on her heels and runs out the door.

I put my head in my hands. What a day: I almost kill my friend, injure my mom, destroy our car, and make Vanna hate me—all in a couple of hours. That must be some kind of record.

This is turning out to be the longest day of my life. I stumble out of the hospital and walk all the way home; that wouldn't be so bad, except that my body really misses the smack. I'm aching, dizzy, and wanting to jump out of my skin.

Finally, I open the door and there's Mom passed out on the couch, a bottle of vodka on the coffee table in front of her. If I'm trying to straighten my life out, why can't she do the same?

I don't feel so well myself. I look out through the glass patio door and see Buzz's paraphernalia lying where he left it when he passed out. I stumble through the room and out onto the patio.

Every cell in my body is pleading for a fix. I see the bag where Buzz left it on the table, still half-full of pure white powder. It seems to reach out and pull me. I sit down, take a piece of foil and heat the powder, then pick up Buzz's syringe and pull the heroin into the clear plastic tube.

What am I doing? This stuff almost killed Buzz. Who knows what's really in that bag? It could kill me. But then, so what if it does? My music career is ruined; my friend is in the hospital, thanks to me; my mom is gonna spend the rest of her life as an insufferable drunk; and worst of all, Vanna has banished me to limbo, forever. There's only one way to get relief.

I take the needle in my fist and jam it in my arm—but I miss the vein. I pull it out, then jab it in again. I stare at the thin steel tube, blood trickling onto my skin where it penetrates my flesh. All I have to do now is shove the plunger down with my thumb.

In my mind's eye, the nightmare returns. I'm in the fog. Vanna is gone. The white woman is drawing me toward her. Her skeletal face leers at me, and I can feel her ice-cold breath. "You're mine Jason, you've given yourself to me, and it's too late to turn back now."

"NO!" I actually shout the words aloud. I tear the needle out of my arm. Blood pours out of my skin as the syringe flies across the patio into the bushes.

With shaking fingers, I punch the speed dial on my cell phone. "Sam—I need help. Can you come over?"

Why Do People with Addictions Relapse?

Addiction is hard to overcome. This doesn't mean an individual with addiction is weak or bad or selfish. Like any other physical disease, addiction has a very real biological component. In other words, no matter how strong and self-disciplined a person may be, addiction has to be addressed within the body as well as the mind.

Research has shown that long-term drug use results in significant changes in brain function, and these changes last long after the individual stops using drugs. This means that the person may never be completely free from his addition, even after he stops using drugs. The drug-induced changes in brain function may have many behavioral consequences, including the compulsion to use drugs despite adverse consequences.

Understanding that addiction has such an important biological component helps explain an individual's difficulty in achieving and maintaining *abstinence*. Psychological stress from work or family problems, social cues (such as meeting individuals from one's drug-using past), or the environment (such as encountering streets, objects, or even smells associated with drug use) can interact with biological factors to make relapses more likely.

This doesn't mean, however, that a person with an addiction is doomed to live out her life controlled by her need for a drug. Research studies indicate that even the most severely addicted individuals can participate actively in treatment, and that active participation is essential to good outcomes.

How Long Does Treatment Last?

Individuals move through drug addiction treatment programs at various speeds, so there is no single predictable length of treatment. However, research indicates that good outcomes depend on sticking with treatment long enough. Generally, for residential or outpatient treatment, participation for less than ninety days isn't long enough to do much good. For methadone maintenance, twelve months of treatment is the minimum, and some opiate-addicted individuals will continue to benefit from methadone maintenance treatment over a period of years.

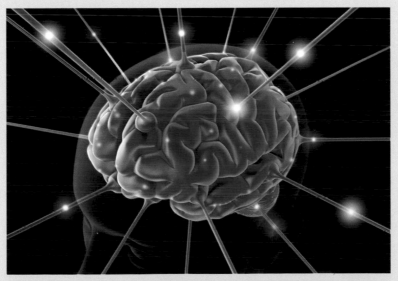

Long-term drug use changes the way the brain functions, which means that for many people, addiction is a permanent condition. That is why people with addictions are often referred to as being in "recovery," rather than "cured"; although they may learn to live sober, they will probably never be completely free of their addictions.

Unfortunately, many people who enter treatment drop out before receiving all the benefits that treatment can provide. Success may require more than one treatment experience. A person with addiction shouldn't become discouraged if she needs several rounds of treatment. Each round may be **cumulative**, bringing her to a stronger place than she was before.

What Are Treatment's Goals?

In addition to stopping drug use, the goal of treatment is to return the individual to his family, workplace, and community as a functioning member. Treatment success is often measured by such factors as levels of

Crime and drug addiction are connected; when addiction is treated, crime rates go down as well.

criminal behavior, family functioning, employability, and medical condition.

How Successful Are Most Treatment Programs?

Overall, treatment of addiction is as successful as treatment of other **chronic** diseases, such as diabetes, **hypertension**, and asthma. According to several studies, drug treatment reduces drug use by 40 to 60 percent, and it significantly decreases criminal activity during and after treatment. For example, a study of therapeutic community treatment for drug offenders found that addiction treatment reduced arrests for violent and nonviolent criminal acts by 40 percent or more. Methadone treatment has been shown to decrease criminal behavior by as much as 50 percent.

Research also shows that drug addiction treatment reduces the risk of HIV infection and that interventions to prevent HIV are much less costly than treating HIV-related illnesses. Treatment can improve the prospects for employment, with gains of up to 40 percent after treatment.

Although these effectiveness rates hold in general, individual treatment outcomes depend on the extent and nature of the individual's addiction, how good a match the treatment is with the individual's needs, and how committed the individual is to the treatment process.

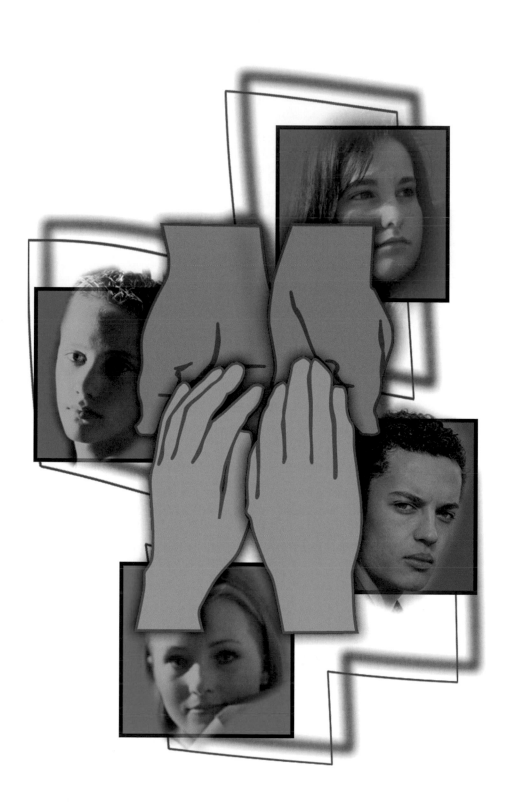

Chapter 8
Showtime

t's almost time to go on stage and this guy from another band comes up and says, "Hey Jason, want to smoke a joint before you go on?" It's amazing, but after five months of being clean, I still have to process that question. I recall the weeks I spent in detox at Seacliff Recovery Center, the countless NA meetings, the innumerable times I've been tempted to go back to the dope.

"No thanks," I tell him finally.

We walk onto the stage. My new bass player, Jose, is grinning and ready to start. On the other side of me is Theo, with his fingers resting on a Kurzwell keyboard.

They're both straight-edge, and happy to be in a drug-free band.

A voice calls out behind me: "Let's rock this joint, Jason!" I turn and grin at Stevie. On the head of his bass drum is the name of our new group—*Second Chance.*

I count off, "One-two-three!" Stevie hits the top drums with a staccato rhythm. I fan the Fender as Theo taps the keys and Jose starts slapping strings. It's amazing: we're all in the same groove! I can feel the sound waves pulsating on my chest, all these instruments sounding as one. I don't think I've ever played so tight yet so inspired.

The crowd is on its feet and moving. Looking out, I see an ocean full of heads, all popping up and down to the sounds pouring out from our instruments. The sound, the crowd, the light show, all move together like one huge heart beating with joy.

There's this little kid just a few feet from the stage; he's moving his skinny frame and looking at me with this shining face like he just saw sunshine for the first time in his life. I wonder, is this the little guy I've been playing for all along, the snot-faced kid with a messed-up home who can find healing from our tunes?

Then I look a little deeper into the crowd and I miss a beat. *She's here*—Vanna. I look down at the monitor in front of me because I can't bear to look at her face. Twice

I've seen disapproval in those eyes; I don't think I can take that again.

I turn around to face Stevie so I won't have to look toward Vanna. Stevie smiles like a guy who's just won the lottery, and his thick arms fly all over that drum set, sticks twirling in his fingers like some hotshot gunslinger in the Old West. I improvise, playing up and down the scale, with the rest of the guys following along. We riff off each other, making sounds like I've never heard before. It's amazing what I can do when all my brain cells are working. The crowd cheers, and I turn around again to look at them. They're going bonkers; they love every note. All those times in the past when I've played stoned I never felt as great as I do tonight.

I can't put off looking at Vanna forever. My hands still fly over the frets as I glance toward her. Once again, the world narrows to a single spot; in my mind's eye there is just one woman on this dance floor. I zoom in on her face . . . and then she puts her hand to her lips and blows me a kiss. I grin.

Suddenly, the world is filled with a million possibilities.

Addiction is a complex disease, regardless of the substance involved, with the potential to disrupt every part of a user's life. Treatment options need to address a broad spectrum of issues, not just the medical component: family relationships, friendships, jobs, housing, school, other health issues, mental health, nutrition, and more should all be looked at. It's a process that will take time.

People who successfully conquer withdrawal symptoms and become substance free are said to be in remission. These individuals are extremely vulnerable to temptations to use the substance again during the first twelve months following withdrawal, however,

Treatment is often a long and challenging process.

All members of a family, both young and old, can offer support to an individual who is battling an addiction.

and any use of the substance can reinstate the cycle of dependence.

Individuals are not ready for treatment until they recognize that they have a substance-related disorder. Often family members, friends, and medical professionals can help the individual realize that the condition exists and needs treatment. Once an individual does understand that he has a substance-related disorder, unless he is involved in a crisis situation (such as an overdose of the substance or severe withdrawal symptoms that warrant emergency treatment), it's a good idea to review all of the options for treatment before entering a program.

Some individuals with a substance-related disorder seek treatment either individually or with the support of family and friends. Others are forced into treatment by the courts after being arrested for possession or use of illegal substances. In the past, treatment options for substance-related disorders were limited to "cold turkey"—simply discontinuing use of the substance, but many more options are available today. A person's background, motivation, and system of support are all important factors to consider when determining the ideal approach to treatment for that person.

With substance-related disorders, it is important to remember that a treatment option that leads to

Each person is unique, and treatment plans must be designed for individual needs.

lasting remission for one person may not work for another. Treatment must be tailored to meet the needs of the individual. A good first step in the treatment of a substance-related disorder is for the individual to obtain a physical examination and a psychiatric assessment. Some psychiatric medications react with others, so it is important for the physician to obtain a history that includes all the medications an individual is already taking. A psychiatric assessment is necessary to determine if there may be underlying causes for substance abuse—anxiety or depression, for example—that also warrant treatment.

Often a combination of therapies is used in recovery from a substance-related disorder, including behavioral and **vocational education**, as well as psychiatric medications. Some psychiatric drug treatments can be administered by any physician, including general practitioners, as well as psychiatrists. Other psychiatric medications can only be prescribed by physicians who have met specific qualifying requirements. Behavioral therapy is administered by various professionals, including psychiatrists, social workers, and other counselors. Some treatment programs use group therapy sessions that include individuals who are recovering from addiction.

While residential facilities exist, including therapeutic communities, hospitals, group homes, and **halfway houses**, most individuals receive nonresidential treatment. Treatment is usually most intensive in the beginning, while the individual is experiencing withdrawal, and immediately thereafter. This can involve inpatient care or an intensive outpatient program. After successfully helping the individual through **detoxification** and the first few weeks of substance-free living, treatments can be reduced gradually. For some addictive substances, long-term care is needed to maintain remission. Some form of treatment (usually counseling) is often continued for one or two years.

The goal of treatment for substance-related disorders is to end the individual's dependence on the substance and to restore her ability to function appropriately in society. While it is not always possible to achieve 100 percent abstinence from an addictive substance, a reduction in use coupled with an ability to carry out family duties and employment roles is evidence of improvement.

Glossary

abstinence: Restraint from indulging a desire for something.

bipolar disorder: A psychiatric disorder characterized by periods of extreme highs and euphoria alternating with periods of extreme lows.

chronic: Long term or recurring frequently.

cumulative: Gradually building up.

detoxification: To free (as a drug user or an alcoholic) from an intoxicating or an addictive substance in the body or from dependence on or addiction to such a substance.

euphoria: A feeling of great joy, excitement, or well-being.

genes: Basic units of heredity.

halfway houses: Rehabilitative residences designed to help people return to society after release from an institution.

hallucinogen: A substance that causes one to perceive someone or something that is not really there.

hypertension: High blood pressure.

initiatives: Plans or strategies designed to deal with a particular problem.

obsessive-compulsive disorder: A psychiatric disorder characterized by recurring thoughts and the need to act upon them.

oppositional defiant disorder: A psychiatric behavior disorder characterized by aggressiveness and a tendency to purposefully bother and irritate others.

post-traumatic stress disorder: A psychological condition that sometimes affects people who have suffered severe emotional trauma.

schizophrenia: A psychological disorder characterized by a disruption of the concept of reality.

sobriety: Abstinence from the use of drugs or alcohol.

stimulants: Drugs that produce a temporary increase in the functional activity of a body organ.

vocational education: Educational programs designed to provide necessary skills for a job or career.

Further Reading

Babbit, Nikki. *Adolescent Drug & Alcohol Abuse: How to Spot It, Stop It, and Get Help for Your Family.* San Francisco: O'Reilly, 2000.

Bellenir, Karen. *Drug Information for Teens: Health Tips About the Physical and Mental Effects of Substance Abuse.* Detroit, Mich.: Omnigraphics, 2002.

Eller, T. Suzanne. *Real Teens, Real Stories, Real Life.* Tulsa, Okla.: River Oak, 2002.

Graves, Bonnie. *Drug Use and Abuse.* Mankato, Minn.: Capstone Press, 2000.

Ketcham, Katherine. *Teens Under the Influence: The Truth About Kids, Alcohol, and Other Drugs—How to Recognize the Problem and What to Do About It.* New York: Ballantine, 2003.

Masline, Shelagh Ryan. *Drug Abuse and Teens: A Hot Issue.* Berkeley Heights, N.J.: Enslow, 2000.

Packer, Alex J. *Highs! Over 150 Ways to Feel Really, Really Good . . . Without Alcohol or Other Drugs.* New York: Free Spirit Publishing, 2000.

For More Information

Al-Anon/Alateen Family Groups
www.al-anon.alateen.org

Alcohol and Other Drug Information for Teens
www.child.net/drugalc.htm

Canadian Centre on Substance Abuse
www.ccsa.ca

Centers for Disease Control and Prevention (CDC) Adolescent and School Health
www.cdc.gov/nccdphp/dash

D.A.R.E. (Drug Abuse Resistance Education)
www.dare.com

D.E.A.L. (Drug Education and Awareness for Life)
www.deal.org

FOCUS Adolescent Services
www.focusas.com

Go Ask Alice!
Columbia University's Health Question and Answer Internet Service
www.goaskalice.columbia.edu

Habit Smart
www.habitsmart.com

National Center for Tobacco-Free Kids
tobaccofreekids.org

National Clearinghouse for Alcohol and Drug Information (NCADI)
www.health.org

National Institute on Alcohol Abuse and Alcoholism (NIAAA)
www.niaaa.nih.gov

National Institute on Drug Abuse (NIDA)
www.drugabuse.gov

NIDA for Teens
teens.drugabuse.gov

NIDA Mind Over Matter (MOM)
www.nida.nih.gov/MOM

NIDA on Steroid Abuse
www.steroidabuse.org

Office of National Drug Control Policy (ONDCP)
www.whitehousedrugpolicy.gov

Straight Scoop New Bureau
www.straightscoop.org

StreetDrugs.Org
www.streetdrugs.org

Students Against Destructive Decisions (SADD)
www.saddonline.com

TEEN ANON
www.teen-anon.com

Teen Health Centre (Canada)
www.teenhealthcentre.com

Teenage Addicts Can Recover
www.day-by-day.org

Publisher's note:
The Web sites listed on these pages were active at the time of publication. The publisher is not responsible for Web sites that have changed their addresses or discontinued operation since the date of publication. The publisher will review and update the Web-site list upon each reprint.

Bibliography

Davenport-Hines, Richard. *The Pursuit of Oblivion: A Global History of Narcotics*. New York: Norton, 2002.

Drug Rehab. "Adolescent Substance Abuse." http://www.drug-rehab.com/adolescent-substance-abuse.htm.

Druguse.com. "Teen Addiction." http://www.druguse.com/Teen_addiction_Teen_addiction_6849.html.

E-notes. "Teen Addiction." http://soc.enotes.com/teen-addiction-article.

Hopelinks.net. "Teen Drug Rehab." http://www.hopelinks.net.

Kid's Health. "Dealing with Addiction." http://kidshealth.org/teen/drug_alcohol_getttinghelp/addictions.

NIDA. "Ask Dr. NIDA—Brain & Addiction." http://teens.drugabuse.gov/drnida/drnida_brain1.asp.

NIDA. "The Science Behind Drug Abuse." http://teens.drugabuse.gov.

Teen Drug Abuse. "Talking to Teens About Addiction." http://www.teendrugabuse.us/teen_addiction.html.

Volpicelli, Joseph, and Maia Szalavitz. *Recovery Options: The Complete Guide*. New York: John Wiley & Sons, 2000.

Index

addiction
    definition 48
    diagnosing 50–51
    effects on the body
        34–41
    reasons 20–27
    relapses 106
    treatment 83–87, 96–99,
        107–109, 114–118
alcohol
    effects of 34–38
    family influence 22–24
    peer influence 24–25
Alcoholics Anonymous 32,
45, 96
Attention Deficit
Hyperactivity Disorder
(ADHD) 34, 72

brain
    brain stem 36, 38, 40
    cerebellum 36, 38, 39
    cerebrum 36, 38, 39
    hypothalamus 37, 38, 39
    limbic system 37, 38, 39

cancer 40, 65, 66
Centers for Disease Control
(CDC) 64
cigarettes 20, 48, 65, 69, 87
cocaine 21, 40, 51, 59, 62,
63, 64, 74, 83, 85, 87

depression 7, 34, 71, 117
DXM 73, 74

ecstasy 21, 74, 75
euphoria 25, 71

heroin
    addictiveness of 61–62
    effects of 59–60
    methods of use 60
HIV 7, 60, 109

inhalants 69, 70

marijuana 21, 59, 67, 68, 69
morphine 59, 60, 71

Narcotics Anonymous 45, 46,
47, 55, 89, 90, 92, 96, 111
National Institute on Drug
Abuse (NIDA) 25, 59, 62,
68
National Survey on Drug
Use and Health 21, 59
neurons 34, 35, 36
neurotransmitters 35, 36,
37, 38, 71, 72, 73
    dopamine 37, 72, 83
    GABA 38, 71, 73
nicotine 37, 49, 64, 65, 68,
86, 87

opium 59, 71
over-the-counter drugs
(OTCs) 73

pain relievers 70, 71
prescription drugs 21, 73

raves 74, 75

sedatives 70, 72, 73, 83
steroids 25, 74
stimulants 25, 63, 70, 72
Substance Abuse and
Mental Health Services
Administration (SAMHSA)
20, 70

tobacco 21, 22, 25, 64
tranquilizers 70, 71, 72, 73

withdrawal 62, 72, 83, 84,
87, 114, 115, 117

Picture Credits

Dolgatshjov, Lev–Fotolia: p. 49
Hunton, Philip–Fotolia: p. 108
iStockphoto:
      Aral, Orguz: p. 38
      Blain, Max: p. 41
      Brown, Marc: p. 67
      Davis, David: p. 23
      Fossier, Pascal: p. 114
      Hafemann, Alexander: p. 63
      Laskowski, Marcin: p. 35
      Lombard, Shaun: p. 68
      Pelletier, Marcel: p. 61
      Tanir, Kutay: p. 48
      Terekhov, Igor: p. 58
      Yakobchuk, Vasily: p. 37
Jupiter Images: pp. 84, 85, 97, 115
Ktsdesign: p. 107
Neoblues: p. 116
Sorokin, Nikolai–Fotolia: p. 65
Stanford University, Amy Feldman: p. 86
Trojanowski, Tomasz–Fotolia: pp. 20, 24
Turnaeva, Iana–Fotolia: p. 26

To the best knowledge of the publisher, all other images are in the public domain. If any image has been inadvertently uncredited, please notify Harding House Publishing Service, Vestal, New York 13850, so that rectification can be made for future printings.

Authors

Kenneth McIntosh is a freelance writer living in northern Arizona with his family. He has written two dozen educational books, and taught at junior high, high school, and community college levels.

Phyllis Livingston has her master's degree in special education. She has worked with a wide variety of teenagers with various psychiatric disorders, including depression and anxiety.

Series Consultants

Sharon Levy, MD, MPH received her MD from New York University School of Medicine and completed her residency at NYU Med Ctr/Bellevue Hospital. She was later awarded a Dyson Fellowship at Children's Hospital Boston. She currently works as an Assistant in Medicine in the General Pediatrics department of the Children's Hospital Boston (CHB), where she also is director of the Adolescent Substance Abuse Program (ASAP). In addition, Dr. Levy serves as an instructor in Pediatrics for Harvard Medical School. Dr. Levy's research focuses on development of drug use treatment strategies for adolescent patients that can be used in the ambulatory medical setting. In previous work she examined physicians' knowledge, practices and attitudes regarding drug testing of adolescent patients and the use of home drug testing by parents of adolescent children.

Cindy Croft, M.A.Ed., is the Director of the Center for Inclusive Child Care (CICC) at Concordia University, St. Paul, MN. The CICC is a comprehensive resource network for promoting and supporting inclusive early childhood and school-age programs and providers with Project EXCEPTIONAL training and consultation, and other resources at www.inclusivechildcare. org. In addition to working with the CICC, Ms. Croft is on the faculty at Concordia University and Minneapolis Community and Technical College.

DATE DUE